understanding
MACROECONOMICS
For NCEA Level Three
EXTERNALS/INTERNALS

Dan Rennie

Workbook
Teacher
RESOURCE

NELSON
A Cengage Company

Australia • Brazil • Mexico • Singapore • United Kingdom • United States

Understanding Macroeconomics for NCEA L3 Teacher Resource
1st Edition
Dan Rennie

Typeset by : *Book*NZ

Any URLs contained in this publication were checked for currency during the production process. Note, however, that the publisher cannot vouch for the ongoing currency of URLs.

Acknowledgement
Thanks to the Reserve Bank Of New Zealand and Statistics New Zealand for their assistance and use of the images and text for various Macroeconomics indicators on Price stability, 90 day bank bill rates, Real Gross Domestic Product, Employment and unemployment, Current Account Balance and the Trade Weighted Index.

For product information and technology assistance,
in Australia call **1300 790 853**;
in New Zealand call **0800 449 725**

For permission to use material from this text or product, please email **aust.permissions@cengage.com**

National Library of New Zealand Cataloguing-in-Publication Data
A catalogue record for this book is available from the National Library of New Zealand

ISBN 978 0 17 043813 1

Cengage Learning Australia
Level 7, 80 Dorcas Street
South Melbourne, Victoria Australia 3205

Cengage Learning New Zealand
Unit 4B Rosedale Office Park
331 Rosedale Road, Albany, North Shore 0632, NZ

For learning solutions, visit **cengage.co.nz**

Printed in Singapore by 1010 Printing Group Limited
1 2 3 4 5 6 7 22 21 20 19 18

Contents

For more information:

Email: nz.sales@cengage.com

Website: www.cengage.co.nz.

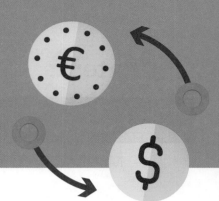

INTRODUCTION

Understanding Macroeconomics has been written for students who are studying Economics at Level Three.

It is a self-supporting workbook which provides the precise economic terms and questions to develop skills that students need to acquire.

Economics is an academic subject and students need to have economic ideas and language as set out in the prescription rather than rely on common knowledge or skills learned in other subjects. This book provides a multitude of activities, sometimes repeated, to encourage answering-precision and to discourage ambiguity.

Understanding Macroeconomics should not be used in isolation but rather in conjunction with text books, classroom notes and assignments. It can be used as either a source of homework or revision but it is mainly designed to provide teaching activities for the year's course.

My hope is that this workbook of activities for the complete course will save teachers time in writing, preparing and copying activities, while providing students with hours of successful work and study.

Dan Rennie

Notes to the student

1   Do all the exercises set by your teacher, making sure you mark these accurately and correct any errors. Do not be afraid of making mistakes. Learn from your mistakes.

2   Ask questions and ask for assistance to questions or topics that you have difficulty with; it is the only way to understand the topics of which you are unsure.

3   Model solutions to all exercises are in the Teacher's Guide.

4   Work is the key to success.

5   Good luck.

   ISBN: 9780170438131

Exam hints

Preparation

Prepare for the exam by completing all exericises in this book, doing old papers or the written questions and the multiple choice questions on **www.eLearneconomics.com**.

In the exam

- Use appropriate economic language, examples and terms in your answers.

- Make accurate references in your answers to the resource material and/or graphs drawn, i.e., provide details in your descriptions, such as figures or names of individuals/firms/products.

- Take care and construct well-labelled, accurate graphs (with a title, graduated scales) using a ruler to plot curves. Refer to these graphs explicitly in your explanations, e.g., D1 to D2, P to P'.

- Write structured answers that link ideas, keep your answers on track and do not contradict what you have written.

- Read questions carefully and add reasons, causes and effects in your explanations.

- Flow-on effects need to be valid, explained in full and kept in context with the event that led to it, rather than a restatement of the initial event itself.

- Attempt all questions.

- Present answers in a legible form.

- Use a pen (not a pencil) on your script to ensure answers are clear.

- Do not use abbreviations or text language because these are not appropriate in a formal exam.

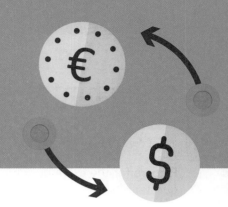

Macroeconomics

Macroeconomics is the study of the economy as a whole rather than individual consumers, individual producers and individual markets. Macroeconomics is concerned with changes in aggregate demand and aggregate supply and the impact that these changes have on employment, price stability, economic growth and the current account. **Aggregate demand (AD)** is total demand in an economy and is comprised of household consumption spending (C), investment spending by firms (I), government spending (G) and net exports (X – M). When there is an increase in a component of aggregate demand (C or I or G or Net exports) this will stimulate economic activity and is likely to result in greater employment, economic growth and inflationary pressures. **Aggregate supply (AS)** is total production of all firms in the economy. If there is an increase in aggregate supply because the productivity of workers increases then the economy will experience economic growth because more goods and services are produced, as output increases firms will need to hire additional workers to produce this output resulting in a decrease in unemployment, and there will be a decrease in inflationary pressures in the economy.

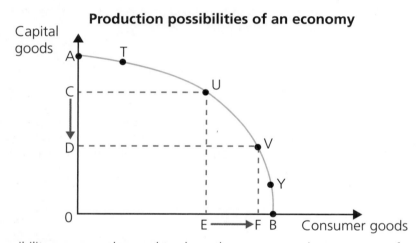

Production possibilities of an economy

A production possibility curve can be used to show the current maximum output of an economy based on the assumption that there are only two goods, fixed resources and a given level of technology. Resources are limited and are used to produce either consumer goods (purchased by households for immediate use e.g., clothes, food, cars) or capital goods (man-made items of capital equipment used to produce other goods and services, e.g., tools, machinery). In the diagram, the maximum potential output (productive capacity) initially is any point on the frontier AB. Full employment would be represented as a point on the frontier, while a point inside would indicate that there is unemployment.

In a fully employed economy a decision to divert resources to produce additional consumer goods can only occur if fewer capital goods are produced. The following analysis illustrates this. The decision to produce more consumer goods from position OE to position OF, results in a fall in production of capital goods of OC to OD. Overall the output of capital goods CD is lost because the resources used to produce capital are now used to produce the additional consumer goods. The decision of an economy to produce more consumer goods (shifting from position U to position V) will result in a higher standard of living now. However future standards of living and output of an economy may increase only gradually. The reason is that as capital goods are not replaced or become obsolete, machinery and equipment will wear out and productivity will decline, causing likely future output to increase slowly or decrease.

Question: Production possibility

1 Compare and contrast the impact of present consumption on growth.

In your answer you should:

- Use a production possibility curve and explain the opportunity cost of present consumption in terms of economic growth.
- Explain how present consumption can positively affect growth.
- Explain how present consumption can negatively affect growth.

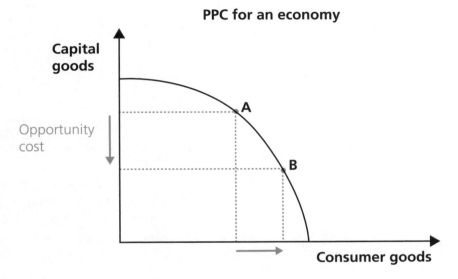

PPC for an economy

A production possibility curve shows the maximum possible output for an economy. If an economy consumes more consumer goods, point B, then there will be a decrease in capital goods (shown and labelled as the opportunity cost) and, therefore, a decrease in economic growth in the future. Growth can be positively affected because if there is an increase in present consumption, firms will find stock levels falling as sales increase, therefore production will increase, resulting in economic growth. OR if present consumption decreases, then more capital goods are produced so there is likely to be more growth in the future.

Growth can be negatively affected because if present consumption increases, there will be less saving so less funds are available for investment. Less investment will mean less growth in the future. OR an increase in present consumption means fewer capital goods are produced so there will be less growth in the future.

Price stability

Inflation in New Zealand

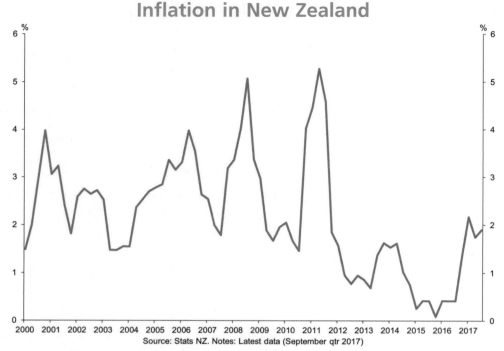

Source: Stats NZ. Notes: Latest data (September qtr 2017)

The Consumers Price Index (CPI) measures changes to the prices of the consumer items New Zealand households buy, and provides a measure of household inflation. Inflation is the term used to describe a rise of average prices through the economy. It means that money is losing its value.

Under the current Policy Targets Agreement (PTA) the Reserve Bank is required to keep annual increases in the CPI between 1 and 3 percent on average over the medium term, with a focus on keeping future average inflation near the 2 percent target midpoint.

Source: Statistics New Zealand

Changes in the general (average) price level are measured by changes in the Consumer Price Index (CPI). An increase in the Consumer Price Index will indicate an increase in the general (average) price level, which is **inflation**. A decrease in the Consumer Price Index will indicate a fall in the general (average) price level, which is **deflation**. **Disinflation** is the term given to the situation where there is a rise in the general (average) price level but by a smaller percentage than the previous time period. Disinflation is a fall in the rate of inflation.

Price stability is the goal of government to avoid long periods of inflation or deflation to keep prices stable so that money can maintain its purchasing power over time.Therefore, governments agree that some inflation in an economy is desirable. In New Zealand, the Governor of the Reserve Bank is charged with keeping inflation between 1% and 3% (on average over the medium term) as outlined in its Policy Target Agreement (PTA).

A large increase in the rate of inflation can have a detrimental effect on various groups. The real income of low income households or those on fixed incomes whose incomes fail to keep up with the increase in the general price level, will fall. The purchasing power of their income falls and they can buy less than previously. Generally, high rates of inflation can harm exporters because their goods and services are less price competitive and therefore more difficult to sell. Importers can benefit from high rates of inflation because their goods and services are relatively more price competitive than those produced or provided by local (domestic) firms. Overall firms may struggle and close down with a resulting increase in unemployment (decrease in employment). Also, as export receipts fall and import payments increase the balance of payments current account will deteriorate (worsen), creating a greater deficit or smaller surplus.

A decrease in the general price level (deflation) can also be viewed as undesirable because it may be a sign that the economy is heading towards a recession. In times of deflation consumption spending may decrease because households delay spending in the hope that prices will fall further. As consumption spending falls firms' stock levels build up and they cut back production. Part of cutting back production will result in fewer workers needed leading to an increase in unemployment.

    ISBN: 9780170438131

Questions: Price stability

90-day bank bill rates and Official Cash Rate

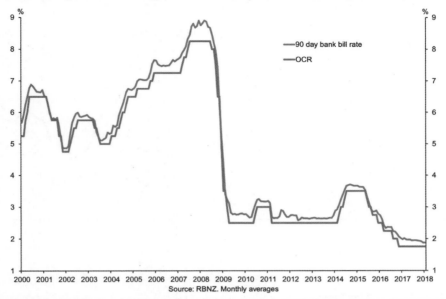

Source: RBNZ. Monthly averages

The Reserve Bank uses the Official Cash Rate (OCR) as its tool for controlling inflation. By setting the OCR, the Reserve Bank is able to influence short-term interest rates such as the 90-day bank bill rate.

Source: RBNZ

1 What is meant by the term price stability?
Explain why both inflation and deflation are undesirable.

Price stability is the goal of government to avoid long periods of inflation or deflation to keep prices stable so that money can maintain its purchasing power over time. In New Zealand, the Governor of the Reserve Bank is charged with keeping inflation between 1% and 3% (on average over the medium term) as outlined in its Policy Target Agreement (PTA).

Inflation is an increase in the general price level of a nation over a period of time usually a year. A large increase in the rate of inflation can have a detrimental effect on various groups. The real income of low income households or those on fixed incomes whose incomes fail to keep up with the increase in the general price level, will fall. The purchasing power of their income falls and they can buy less than previously. Generally, high rates of inflation can harm exporters because their goods and services are less price competitive and therefore more difficult to sell. Importers can benefit from high rates of inflation because their goods and services are relatively more price competitive than those produced or provided by local (domestic) firms. Overall firms may struggle and close down with a resulting increase in unemployment. Also, as export receipts fall and import payments increase the balance of payments current account will deteriorate (worsen), creating a greater deficit or smaller surplus.

A decrease in the general price level (deflation) can also be viewed as undesirable because it may be a sign that the economy is heading towards a recession. In times of deflation consumption spending may decrease because households delay spending in the hope that prices will fall further. As consumption spending falls firms' stock levels build up and they cut back production. Part of cutting back production will result in fewer workers needed leading to an increase in unemployment.

Economic growth
Real Gross Domestic Product
(annual average % change)

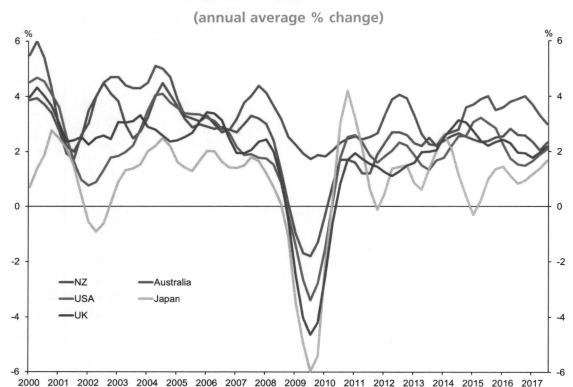

Source: Stats NZ, Haver.

Gross domestic product (GDP) represents the value of all goods and services produced in New Zealand. Real GDP is New Zealand's official measure of economic growth.

Source: Statistics New Zealand

Nominal GDP refers to the value of output at current market prices. Nominal GDP exaggerates economic growth when prices rise due to inflation. The nominal value of national output may increase without an increase in the real output of goods and services.

Real GDP refers to the nominal GDP adjusted for price changes relative to some base year. It is the changes in real GDP that allow for measuring economic growth in real terms and determining increases in the standard of living. When there is an increase in real output GDP, this means that an economy has produced more goods and services than the previous year and the economy has experienced economic growth.

As an economy expands, employment increases because firms hire additional workers to increase the output needed to satisfy the increase in demand, or they will use existing staff and pay overtime. There will be fewer redundancies in the workplace because fewer firms close down. Also, more firms will start up, because the perceived risks of operating a business in a buoyant environment are lower. The increase in business confidence will lead to increased investment because the chances of the venture being successful and profitable are higher. Overall, in an expanding economy, fewer individuals will lose jobs and, with new firms hiring staff, the unemployment rate in the economy will decrease. Greater job opportunities for some workers arise because of shortages of certain skills in some sectors or industries.

For the government, economic growth is desirable because it brings in increasing revenues from a given structure of tax rates. It means that more and better roads, schools, hospitals and other social services can be provided without resorting to raising the rates of taxation. Growth is an objective of government economic policy because it is one of the keys to higher standards of living. Economic growth makes it easier for the government to carry out policies of income redistribution and achieve greater equity (fairness) of income distribution.

       ISBN: 9780170438131

Questions: Economic growth

1 What is the difficulty in using changes in the nominal value of GDP to measure economic growth?

Nominal GDP exaggerates economic growth when prices rise due to inflation. The nominal value of national output may increase without an increase in the real output of goods and services.

2 What is economic growth and explain the impact of growth on employment?

When there is an increase in real output GDP, this means that an economy has produced more goods and services than the previous year and the economy has experienced economic growth. As an economy expands, employment increases because firms hire additional workers to increase the output needed to satisfy the increase in demand, or they will use existing staff and pay overtime. There will be fewer redundancies in the workplace because fewer firms close down. Also, more firms will start up, because the perceived risks of operating a business in a buoyant environment are lower. The increase in business confidence will lead to increased investment because the chances of the venture being successful and profitable are higher. Overall, in an expanding economy, fewer individuals will lose jobs and, with new firms hiring staff, the unemployment rate in the economy will decrease. Greater job opportunities for some workers arise because of shortages of certain skills in some sectors or industries.

3 Why is economic growth an objective of government?

For the government, economic growth is desirable because it brings in increasing revenues from a given structure of tax rates. It means that more and better roads, schools, hospitals and other social services can be provided without resorting to raising the rates of taxation. Growth is an objective of government economic policy because it is one of the keys to higher standards of living. Economic growth makes it easier for the government to carry out policies of income redistribution and achieve greater equity (fairness) of income distribution.

Employment

The unemployment rate reflects labour market conditions. It measures the proportion of people in the labour force who are unemployed. Unemployment is defined as being without paid work, where a person was available for and actively seeking work. The labour force includes all people who are employed and unemployed.

Source: Statistics New Zealand

Employment and unemployment in New Zealand

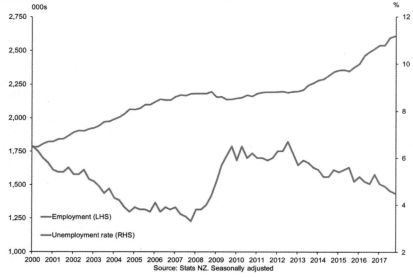

Source: Stats NZ. Seasonally adjusted

Employment and unemployment

In an economy a government would want to increase employment and decrease unemployment, ideally it would like to be as close to full employment as possible. However, most governments accept that there will always be some degree of short-term unemployment in an economy because there are those who are temporarily between jobs and those entering the labour force for the first time or individuals re-entering the labour force (**frictional unemployment**).

Of more concern for a government are those individuals who are **structurally unemployed** as a result of permanent or long-term changes in the structure of the economy. This type of unemployment is caused by changes in technology or final demand where different types of labour are required. Individuals who are structurally unemployed need to adapt, learn new skills or retrain to gain the skills that coincide with the current requirements of employers to be able to find employment.

When an economy slows down, demand begins to fall. A decrease in consumption spending will impact on firms because as households demand fewer goods and services, firms will decrease production. As part of decreasing production firms will need to use fewer resources and employ fewer workers, lay workers off or make some workers redundant. Therefore, a downturn in economic activity (ie, either a recession or depression) causes **demand deficient (cyclical) unemployment** to occur. It will see almost all industries in an economy affected to varying degrees, this type of unemployment will be at its worst in the trough section of the trade cycle and may result in mass unemployment. A government will look to stimulate economic activity by lowering interest rates or running an expansionary fiscal policy (an operating deficit).

Changes in the methods of production can lead to the use of labour-saving machines and make some workers redundant or in need of retraining to acquire the necessary skills to remain employed at the same location. When business expectations of profit or business confidence falls, the level of private investment decreases and fewer job opportunities are provided. Anything that causes uncertainty in an economy can affect business confidence and producers tend to forgo or reduce the expansion or replacement of capital assets. Global events (wars, an economic downturn), inflation or inflationary expectations could be a cause of such uncertainty.

Statistics on unemployment need to be treated with caution as they may both magnify or understate the problem. Counting unemployed as those individuals temporarily between jobs or those who are unemployed but actually work in the underground (black) economy may overestimate unemployment. Discouraged workers who give up looking for employment but do not register as unemployed may underestimate figures on unemployment.

       ISBN: 9780170438131

Questions: Employment and unemployment

1 Explain what the goal for most governments is in regard to employment, and why frictional unemployment is of less concern for a government than structural unemployment.

In an economy a government would want to increase employment and decrease unemployment to keep unemployment low, ideally it would like to be as close to full employment as possible. However, most governments accept that there will always be some degree of short-term unemployment in an economy because there are those who are temporarily between jobs and those entering the labour force for the first time or individuals re-entering the labour force (frictional unemployment).

Of more concern for a government are those individuals who are structurally unemployed as a result of permanent or long-term changes in the structure of the economy. This type of unemployment is caused by changes in technology or final demand where different types of labour are required. Individuals who are structurally unemployed need to adapt, learn new skills or retrain to gain the skills that coincide with the current requirements of employers to be able to find employment.

2 What is cyclical (demand-deficient) unemployment and when is it likely to be at its worst?

Demand-deficient (cyclical) unemployment occurs when there is not enough demand to employ all those who want to work. It will vary with the trade cycle, when the economy is booming, there will be lots of demand and so firms will be employing large numbers of workers. When an economy slows down, demand begins to fall. A decrease in consumption spending will impact on firms because as households demand fewer goods and services, firms will decrease production. As part of decreasing production firms will need to use fewer resources and employ fewer workers, lay workers off or make some workers redundant. Therefore, a downturn in economic activity (ie, either a recession or depression) causes demand-deficient (cyclical) unemployment to occur. It will see almost all industries in an economy affected to varying degrees, this type of unemployment will be at its worst in the trough section of the trade cycle and may result in mass unemployment. A government will look to stimulate economic activity by lowering interest rates or running an expansionary fiscal policy (an operating deficit).

Current account

The Balance of Payments (BoP) statistics set out a country's transactions with the rest of the world. The current account records New Zealand's transactions in goods, services, income, and current transfers with the rest of the world. The current account measures what a country earns offshore minus what it spends offshore.

Source: Statistics New Zealand

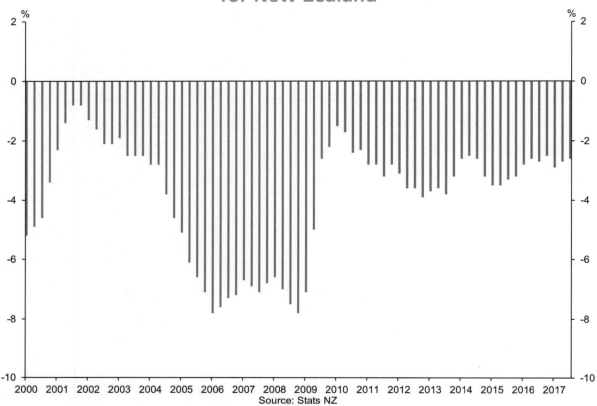

The current account balance

The current account records the difference between export receipts and import payments, a government's objective will be to increase exports and decrease imports. An increase in export receipts and/or a decrease in import payments will see the balance of payments current account improve, a greater surplus or a smaller deficit. A government will look to achieve a balanced current account.

Changes in the current account have a flow-on effect on levels of economic growth, employment and inflation in an economy. If there is an upturn in overseas demand, greater spending on exports means that exporting firms will produce more, earning higher incomes and are likely to employ more staff, which will cause unemployment to fall. Also, it is likely that business confidence will increase and firms will invest (buy new capital) because they view the project as involving less risk and being relatively more profitable. An increase in both consumption spending and investment spending will increase aggregate demand and result in an increase in real output GDP (economic growth). If the economy is close to full employment there will be added inflationary pressures in the economy.

A large persistent current account balance is an important issue for an economy because a current account deficit is funded by borrowing from overseas. It can mean that external (overseas) debt increases and results in increasing foreign ownership of a nation's economic assets. This external debt must be serviced by export income. Overseas funds are attracted into a country when interest rates are relatively high. These high interest rates can have a negative impact on an economy because consumers and producers will be less inclined to borrow and consumption and investment will decrease, therefore real output GDP may fall.

Questions: Current account

1 Explain what the current account is and what a government will hope to achieve in relation to the current account.

The current account records the difference between export receipts and import payments, a government's objective will be to increase exports and decrease imports. An increase in export receipts and/or a decrease in import payments will see the balance of payments current account improve, a greater surplus or a smaller deficit. A government will look to achieve a balanced current account.

2 Explain the impact increased trade might have on the economy.

Changes in the current account have a flow-on effect on levels of economic growth, employment and inflation in an economy. If there is an upturn in overseas demand, greater spending on exports means that exporting firms will produce more, earning higher incomes and are likely to employ more staff, which will cause unemployment to fall. Also, it is likely that business confidence will increase and firms will invest (buy new capital) because they view the project as involving less risk and being relatively more profitable. An increase in both consumption spending and investment spending will increase aggregate demand and result in an increase in real output GDP (economic growth). If the economy is close to full employment there will be added inflationary pressures in the economy.

3 Explain why a large current account balance is an important issue for a country.

A large persistent current account balance is an important issue for an economy because a current account deficit is funded by borrowing from overseas. It can mean that external (overseas) debt increases and results in increasing foreign ownership of a nation's economic assets. This external debt must be serviced by export income. Overseas funds are attracted into a country when interest rates are relatively high. These high interest rates can have a negative impact on an economy because consumers and producers will be less inclined to borrow and consumption and investment will decrease, therefore real output GDP may fall.

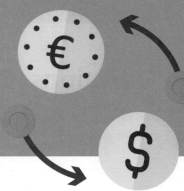

The circular flow model

The circular flow model (households and firms)

The circular flow diagram is an economic model that shows how the household, firms, government and overseas sectors are interrelated, and are all interdependent on each other. The model is based on several assumptions. We group consumers into households and assume that households own all resources. We group producers into firms.

A producer (firm) is any person or organisation that uses resources (natural, human or capital goods) to create goods and services

Consumers are individuals or households (a group of individuals) that consume (use) goods and services produced by producers (firms or businesses).

Circular flow: Household and firms

Real Flow: Resources (F.O.P)

Real Flow: Goods and Services

Households → Firms

$ Money Flow: Consumption Spending (C)

$ Money Flow: Incomes (Y)

Real (physical) flows in the model are factors of production (resources) and goods and services. The real flow of resources (inputs) owned by households are used by firms to produce goods and provide services. Goods (commodities) are objects (or items) that have a physical presence, such as clothes and food. Services are what someone does for you, such as the work of a mechanic or doctor.

Money flows in the model are those that finance the flows of resources, goods and services. Firms pay households' incomes (Y) for the resources they supply. Households use this income to purchase the goods and services they desire from firms, this is termed consumption spending (C). As an economy grows (expands) it will influence the flows in the circular flow model. If consumers' demand for goods and services increases, then firms will require additional inputs (resources) to produce the increased output required. In turn, firms will pay households more for the inputs used and households' incomes will rise.

Savings and financial institutions

A household can either spend or save the income it receives. **Consumption spending (C)** is household spending on goods and services and is likely to increase when incomes rise. The sacrificing of present consumption is **savings (S)** because it represents income not spent. The level of savings a household has will depend on several factors including interest rates, expectations about the future and attitudes towards

Circular flow and financial institutions

$ Consumption spending (C)

Households → Firms

$Incomes (Y)

$ Savings (S) → Financial Intermediaries → **$ Investment (I)**

thrift. Individuals may save more if they are concerned about the future and desire to have funds for an emergency, such as an unexpected bill for repairs to a house or car. As interest rates increase individuals are likely to save more because they are receiving a higher return on funds put aside to use later.

Savings are made with financial institutions who use these funds to make advances (or loans) to firms, who purchase capital goods. The spending by firms on capital goods is termed **investment (I)**. Capital (producer) goods are man-made goods used in the production of other goods and services, for example, tools, machinery.

 ISBN: 9780170438131

Financial intermediaries facilitate the interaction between households and firms. Investment spending by firms will often involve firms borrowing. A financial institution can only make funds available for investment once they have collected deposits (savings) from households. If the level of savings increases then there are more funds available for investment. This, however, does not necessarily mean that increased investment will take place, for several reasons. Financial institutions may find it difficult to find credit worthy firms to make advances (loans) to, or firms do not wish to invest because they are not confident about the future. A lower level of savings means that there are less funds available for firms to borrow to invest in capital equipment, because financial institutions do not have the funds available to advance.

The role of government

The government collects direct tax (T) and indirect tax (IT) and spends money on goods and services or provides subsidies to firms. These flows are illustrated on the diagram below.

Circular flow: Role of government

Government tax take (income) and level of spending will change with changes in the level of economic activity. As the economy grows and firms hire additional workers or pay existing workers overtime, then the government will collect more direct tax as employment increases. Also as disposable incomes increase and consumption spending increases then firms will collect more indirect tax (GST) and pass this on to the government. The government will pay less on transfer payments (Tr) because individuals who were unemployed are now able to get a job. **Government spending (G)** may increase as its revenue increases or it may decide to reduce levels of government debt.

If income (direct) tax rates are cut, households disposable income will increase. Households are likely to save more and spend proportionately less on inferior goods and/or necessities, more luxuries will be purchased. Firms are likely to find that sales increase. With greater sales firms are likely to increase production, hire additional workers or pay existing workers overtime. Revenue is likely to increase as will profit. A firm might open a new shop, move to a bigger location or look at bringing expansion plans forward and seeking a loan from a financial institution to invest in new capital items the firm needs. Initially the decrease in income (direct) tax rates might cause government tax revenues to fall. However, in the long run government tax revenue could rise because direct tax receipts increase because firms that hire additional workers, or pay existing workers overtime, now pay tax that was not being paid previously. Tax receipts will also increase if household spending increases and firms collect more indirect tax from GST.

Trade/Overseas

Some economic activity in a country is associated with foreign buyers and sellers. **Export receipts (X)** represent a money flow into a country for goods and services sold to overseas buyers. **Import payments (M)** represent a money flow out of a country for goods and services purchased from overseas producers.

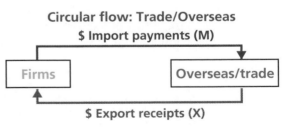

Circular flow: Trade/Overseas

An increase in households' incomes could see an increase in import payments (M) because households decide to take overseas holidays or purchase imported goods and services such as electrical goods or cars. If there is a boom in the global economy, with higher incomes for overseas households, then export receipts can increase, which will have a flow-on effect for producers. Producers may become more confident about the future and move expansion plans forward and invest.

Injections and leakages

When money is taken out from the circular flow of economic activity we call it a leakage (or withdrawal), and when money is put into the circular flow we call it an injection. Injections (J) is an expenditure that does not originate from household and will increase the level of economic activity - investment spending (I), government spending (G) or export receipts (X). Leakages or withdrawals (W) that will decrease the level of economic activity are savings (S), taxes (T) and import payments (M).

1 a Label the missing spaces in the diagram below.

A three-sector circular flow model

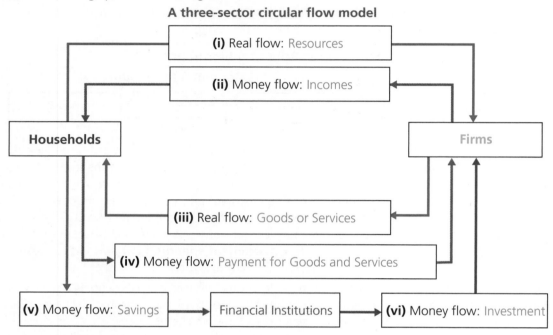

b Describe the difference between incomes and resources.

Incomes are the payments for resources while resources are the factors of production used to produce goods and services.

> Links exist between investment, savings, economic growth and inflation.

c Explain the statement above. In your answer you should:
- Define savings and explain why when interest rates fall it is likely that savings decrease.
- Explain the effect of increased savings on financial institutions.
- Explain how savings may affect economic growth and inflation.

Savings are income not spent. As interest rates fall then saving is likely to decrease because people (households) will be getting a lower return on funds set aside, therefore saving less.

When financial institutions collect greater deposits from household savings they will have greater funds available to lend out to firms for investment.

The increase in savings means more funds for investment. This will increase the ability of firms to invest. This will cause aggregate demand to increase (shift outward) and cause an increase in the general price level (demand-pull inflation) and an increase in real output GDP which is economic growth. Increased investment will improve productivity and productive capacity, resulting in increasing output and economic growth will increase. As the aggregate supply curve shifts outward it will reduce inflationary pressures in the economy.

2 a Explain how savings can result in future growth.

Greater savings makes money available for investment. This results in an increase in capital goods and will result in an increase in production and growth. The production possibility curve will shift outward or move from a point inside the curve to one further out.

b Explain why an increase in savings might not result in future economic growth.

An increase in savings results in less consumption, producers sell less, less profit, cut back production. Increased savings may not be available for borrowing for investment. Less investment, less production. While savings may increase, firms are unwilling to borrow because interest rates are too high or there is a lack of business confidence. Less borrowing for investment, less production.

c Outline some factors that will influence the level of savings.

The level of savings a household has will depend on several factors including interest rates, expectations about the future and attitudes towards thrift. Individuals may save more if they are concerned about the future and desire to have funds for an emergency, such as an unexpected bill for repairs to a house or car. As interest rates increase individuals are likely to save more because they are receiving a higher return on funds put aside to use later.

d If the level of savings increases then there are more funds available for investment. Explain several reasons why investment might not take place.

A financial institution can only make funds available for investment once they have collected deposits (savings) from households. If the level of savings increases then there are more funds available for investment. This, however, does not necessarily mean that increased investment will take place, for several reasons. Financial institutions may find it difficult to find credit worthy firms to make advances (loans) to, or firms do not wish to invest because they are not confident about the future.

Events such as the rugby and rowing world cups and the world orienteering championships increase total economic activity.

3 **a** Explain how events contribute to increased economic activity. In your answer you should:
- State the injection flows in the circular flow model and explain how each injection flow will increase because of events.
- Explain how events will cause economic growth directly and indirectly.

The injection flows in the circular flow model are investment spending (I), government spending or subsidies (G) and export receipts (X).

Investment spending (I) by firms will increase before the events take place so that firms can take the opportunities that will arise when the event is on. Visitors will need a place to stay (accommodation), food and transport, therefore firms in these industries will look to replace old plant and machinery and increase capacity to satisfy additional demand. Because infrastructure needs to be built for these events (stadiums, roading) firms in the construction industry will also increase investment spending.

Government spending (G) will increase because government and local authorities are involved in funding some of the costs of infrastructure. Export receipts (X) will increase as visitors (tourists) and competitors come to participate in or watch the events, they will consume goods and services in New Zealand such as food, accommodation and transport.

A direct effect is the actual spending on the events as they take place, for example, taxis or train trips to the games or spending on merchandise sold during the events. An indirect effect will arise as firms hire additional workers while the events are on or pay existing workers overtime. As their disposable incomes rise then it is likely that consumption spending by households will increase. Both the direct and indirect effects will see AD shift outward and an increase in real output GDP, which is economic growth, as output in the economy increases.

b Complete the table. Tick (✓) the correct column.

Event or situation		Stimulates economic activity	Dampens economic activity
(i)	Direct (income) tax cuts	✓	
(ii)	Lower interest rates	✓	
(iii)	Increased business confidence	✓	
(iv)	An increase in inflationary expectations by households	✓	
(v)	A recession		✓
(vi)	Lower business confidence		✓
(vii)	An expansionary fiscal policy	✓	
(viii)	A government operating deficit	✓	
(ix)	A government operating surplus		✓
(x)	A contractionary fiscal policy		✓
(xi)	Increased interest rates		✓

    ISBN: 9780170438131

4 Use the information in the diagram to answer the questions that follow.

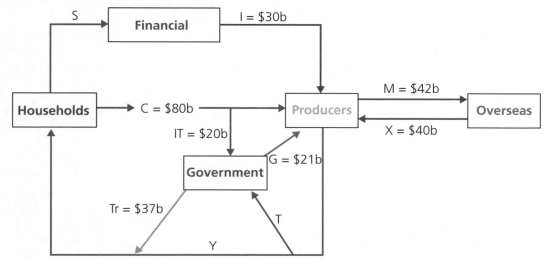

a Give the letter(s) of the flow in the diagram above that best represents the following.

(i)	Export receipts	X	**(vi)**	A firm building a new factory	I
(ii)	Final household consumption expenditure	C	**(vii)**	Import payments	M
(iii)	Compensation to employees	Y	**(viii)**	An individual receives income support	Tr
(iv)	Gross fixed capital formation	I	**(ix)**	Benefit payments to the unemployed	Tr
(v)	Taxes on production	IT	**(x)**	A farmer builds a shed	I

b Indicate if the following money flows are injections (J) or withdrawals (W) in the circular flow model by placing a tick (✓) in the appropriate box.

	Injections (J)	Withdrawals (W)
(i) Government spending (G)	✓	
(ii) Savings (S)		✓
(iii) Investment (I)	✓	
(iv) Firms buying capital	✓	
(v) Taxes (T)		✓
(vi) Export receipts (X)	✓	
(vii) Import payments (M)		✓

c Indicate which money flow best represents the following situations by placing a tick (✓) in the appropriate box.

	C	I	G	X	S	T	M
(i) A business borrows money to buy a new factory.		✓					
(ii) A firm pays indirect tax (GST).						✓	
(iii) A worker deposits some of their income into a term deposit.					✓		
(iv) A student buys lunch.	✓						
(v) An American firm buys New Zealand-made products.				✓			
(vi) A New Zealand tourist on holiday overseas.							✓

A few of New Zealand's trading partners in Europe
are in a downswing phase of the business cycle.

5 Complete **a** and **b** to comprehensively analyse the effect on economic growth of a few of New Zealand's trading partners in Europe being in the downswing phase of the business cycle, and the effect of an increase in consumer confidence.

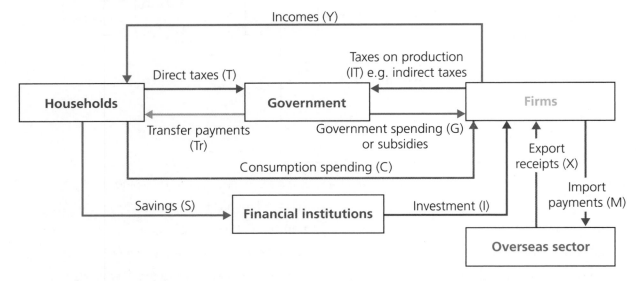

a Explain in detail which money flow would be directly affected by a few of New Zealand's trading partners in Europe being in a downswing phase of the business cycle.

If a few of New Zealand's trading partners in Europe are in a downswing phase of the business cycle the

money flow that is affected is export receipts. Export receipts would decrease because lower incomes

of overseas buyers would result in less demand for New Zealand goods and services.

b Compare and contrast the impact on economic growth of a few of New Zealand's trading partners in Europe being in a downswing phase of the business cycle with the impact of an increase in consumer confidence.

In your answer, refer to the relevant money flows from the circular flow model and explain:

- how a few of New Zealand's trading partners in Europe being in a downswing phase of the business cycle could affect economic growth
- how an increase in consumer confidence could affect economic growth
- the combined impact on economic growth of both these events.

If a few of New Zealand's trading partners in Europe are in the downswing phase of the business cycle they will demand fewer New Zealand goods and services because their income will be lower. As export receipts fall, aggregate demand will shift inward, causing real output GDP to decrease. As less is produced, growth falls.

An increase in consumer confidence will result in an increase in consumption spending which will shift AD outward. This will cause an increase in real output GDP, economic growth.

The combined effect is that the increase in AD from consumer confidence is greater than the decrease in AD from a few of New Zealand's trading partners in Europe. A few nations in Europe are not one of New Zealand's major trading partners so the impact of a decreased demand is likely to be small compared with consumption spending by households. Consumption spending contributes a greater component to AD than does exports. It is likely that increased consumption spending by households will cancel the effect of decreased demand for New Zealand exports from a few trading partners in Europe.

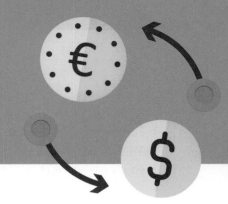

Aggregate demand and aggregate supply

Aggregate demand (AD)

Aggregate demand (AD) is total demand in the economy and is equivalent to national income (Y). The components of aggregate demand are C plus I plus G plus (X – M).

Aggregate demand (AD) is the quantity of national output that is purchased at a given price level and represents the total demand in an economy.

The aggregate demand curve slopes downward to the right – as the price level (PL) increases, the aggregate demand for all goods and services will decrease.

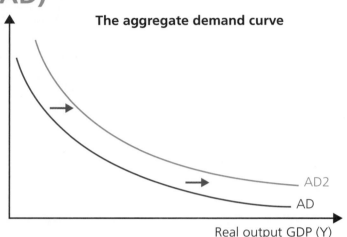

The aggregate demand curve

Price level (PL)

Real output GDP (Y)

AD2

AD

Consumption spending (C)

Consumption spending (C) is household spending (or expenditure) on goods and services. As consumption spending increases aggregate demand will shift outward (to the right). If there is a decrease in direct (income) tax or transfer payments are increased then consumption spending will increase because household disposable incomes (HDI) increase and households can afford more. When interest rates fall there is less incentive for households to save, because they get a lower return and this will discourage savings therefore consumption spending will increase. Also, when interest rates fall then it is possible that households will get a loan to buy items they desire, do renovations to homes or buy a property (home), this will increase consumption spending.

If households are concerned that the general price level is going to increase, then they will buy now, rather than later when goods and services are more expensive. This will cause consumption spending to increase.When migrants arrive in a country they will look to set up homes and are likely to buy whiteware and furniture, consumption spending will increase. There is a wealth effect that can occur when property and house prices increase. Households may be encouraged to borrow more from banks and financial institutions by asking for a loan based on the increased equity they have in their home or property. As borrowed funds are spent on goods and services consumption spending will increase.

Investment spending (I)

Investment spending (I) or capital formation takes place when firms buy capital, for example, a farmer buys a quad bike, a horticulturist builds a dam for irrigation purposes or a manufacturer installs new machinery. As investment spending increases aggregate demand will shift outward (to the right). Businesses are more likely to increase their level of investment spending if they are confident about the prospects of a venture or project being successful. As part of this process of deciding to invest (purchase new capital items) or not, firms will consider the cost of borrowing the funds required (i.e., interest rates), the level of risk involved as well as the profitability of the decision.

As interest rates increase then firms are less likely to invest because the risk is higher and the profitability is reduced because the cost of borrowing funds has increased. Investment spending will fall and decrease aggregate demand.

ISBN: 9780170438131

Government spending (G)

Fiscal policy is the name given to changes in levels of government income (revenue) and expenditure in order to influence the level of economic activity. A government operating (budget) deficit is where government spending exceeds income. This is expansionary fiscal policy which is used during a recession, depression or period of stagnant economic activity. It involves either increasing government spending, increasing transfers or decreasing direct or indirect taxes or both. Expansionary fiscal policy will result in an increase in aggregate demand which will stimulate economic activity.

A government operating (budget) surplus occurs when the government's income is greater than its expenditure. It could involve a decrease in government spending, decreasing transfer payments and increasing both direct and indirect taxes. This contractionary fiscal policy will reduce levels of spending and result in a decrease in aggregate demand which will dampen the level of economic activity.

Net exports (X – M)

 Some economic activity in a country is associated with foreign buyers and sellers. Influences on net exports (exports minus imports) include the state of the global economy, tariffs and exchange rates. Export receipts (X) represent a money flow into a country for goods and services sold to overseas buyers. Exports of goods and services (X) represents an injection into a country's circular flow of income and spending adding to aggregate demand. Import payments (M) represent a money flow out of a country for goods and services purchased from overseas producers. Imports of goods and services (M) represents a leakage or withdrawal from a country's circular flow of income and spending.

Aggregate supply (AS)

Aggregate supply (AS) is total production of all firms in the economy.

The aggregate supply curve shows the real output that firms are willing to supply at each price level.

During a recession, downturn or at low levels of output (on the relatively flat part of the aggregate supply curve or further away from full employment) firms are willing to increase output with a small increase in the price level, because they have idle capacity. The slope

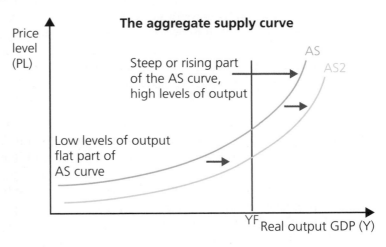

becomes steeper as much larger increases in prices are needed to induce firms to invest or add extra shifts and pay overtime.

In a boom period as the economy approaches capacity, it is more difficult to increase output because there is less spare capacity. There may be hold-ups and bottlenecks, so prices rise. The aggregate supply curve rises as the economy reaches full capacity.

The **full employment (YF)** or long-run aggregate supply curve shows that all resources are fully employed and that firms are working to their capacity. The YF curve will shift outwards when new technology is developed or if new resources are discovered.

Shifts of the aggregate supply curve

A change in the price of inputs (costs of production) used in the production process has an impact on aggregate supply. Unions getting a nominal wage award for workers or increases in the price of power and transportation fees increase the price of inputs used by firms in the production process. As costs of production increase, profits will decrease and the aggregate supply curve will shift inward (to the left).

Some inputs used by firms in production can come from overseas. The price of imported components used by firms in the production process can be dependent on fluctuations in the exchange rate. As an exchange rate depreciates imported components or raw materials are more expensive so costs of production for firms increase. Increased costs decrease profit so the aggregate supply curve shifts inward (to the left) as planned output at each price level falls. If an exchange rate appreciates imported raw materials or components will be cheaper. This will lower costs of production and increase profit so the aggregate supply curve shifts outward (to the right) as planned output increases.

The size of the labour force and net migration have an impact on aggregate supply. The size of the labour force changes as the school leaving age, retirement age or net migration change. As the size of the labour force decreases wages will increase, ceteris paribus. As costs of production increase profits will fall and the aggregate supply curve will shift inward. When migrants arrive in a country they add to the size of the labour force and wages will fall, ceteris paribus. As wages fall, firms' costs of production decrease. As costs of production decrease, profits increase and the aggregate supply curve will shift outward (to the right).

Changes made by the government regarding indirect taxes (GST, VAT), government charges or regulations that impact on firms' costs of production will affect aggregate supply. An indirect tax is a tax collected by a third party and passed on to the government. All businesses pay indirect tax, therefore any change in indirect tax rates has a large impact on aggregate supply because a firm's costs of production either increase or decrease. If the rate of an indirect tax is raised, it will cause firm's costs to increase and profits to decrease. As profits decrease aggregate supply will decrease, with the aggregate supply curve shifting inwards. Introduction by the government of new health and safety laws that require firms to take further measures to ensure workplace safety increases the costs of production for firms. As firms' costs increase, profits decrease and the aggregate supply curve will shift inward.

Productivity is a factor that will cause the aggregate supply curve to shift. Productivity is a measure of the efficiency of the production process and refers to the rate of output. It is a measure of output per unit of input; i.e., output divided by input. Productivity of labour is output per worker, i.e., output divided by the number of workers. It is likely that with improved productivity a firm's costs fall as the production process becomes more efficient, profits will rise and the aggregate supply curve will shift outwards. Productivity of labour (output per worker) can be improved by training workers, greater specialisation by utilising the division of labour or increased use of technology. Higher rates of higher education qualifications result in a better educated workforce that should result in higher levels of output per worker (productivity).

Technological advancements as a consequence of Research and Development can result in newer and faster ways to produce goods and services, the costs of production to firms will decrease for a given quantity of inputs. As productivity levels increase, firms' costs of production fall. Decreased costs increase profits, so firms plan to produce more at each price level thereby shifting the aggregate supply curve to the right (outward).

Some economic conditions or factors will influence both aggregate demand and aggregate supply, for example exchange rates, migration and interest rates. Individuals who join the KiwiSaver scheme in New Zealand or existing members who decide to increase the size of their contribution to the scheme will be increasing their level of savings, therefore consumption spending will decrease which will decrease aggregate demand. Firms in New Zealand must contribute to the KiwiSaver scheme, so costs of production will increase. As firms' costs increase, profits decrease and aggregate supply will shift inward.

      ISBN: 9780170438131

QUESTIONS & TASKS

1 **a** Write each word or phrase in the correct column in the table: costs of production, technology, income tax, sales tax, GST, interest rates, transfer payments, level of workers' productivity, cost of imported raw materials, government spending, savings, expectations about inflation, level of labour force, a wage award, net exports, business confidence, migration, exchange rates.

Shifts AD	Shifts AS
income tax	costs of production
interest rates	technology
transfer payments	sales tax
government spending	GST
savings	level of workers' productivity
expectations about inflation	cost of imported raw materials
net exports	interest rates
business confidence	level of labour force
migration	a wage award
exchange rates	migration
	exchange rates

b List the components of aggregate demand. Standard abbreviations are acceptable.

AD = C + I + G + (X – M)

c Indicate the direction the aggregate demand curve will shift for the situations given in the table below.

	Situation	Direction that AD shifts inward or outward
(i)	Income tax rates decrease	outward
(ii)	A rise in business confidence	outward
(iii)	A larger than expected budget surplus	inward
(iv)	Interest rates rise as the OCR is raised	inward
(v)	The government announces that GST will increase in six months time	outward
(vi)	A fall in business confidence	inward
(vii)	Transfer payments are increased	outward
(viii)	Net exports $1 912m surplus	outward
(ix)	The Reserve Bank Governor lowers the OCR and interest rates fall	outward
(x)	Contractionary fiscal policy	inward
(xi)	A net migration loss	inward
(xii)	A budget surplus	inward
(xiii)	A large increase in households starting to save for their retirement	inward
(ix)	Consumers go on a spending spree fearing price rises in the future	outward

2 **a** Indicate which direction the aggregate supply curve will shift for the situations given.

	Situation	Direction that AS curve will shift inward or outward
(i)	New technology is developed	outward
(ii)	Workers' productivity falls as machinery wears out and depreciates	inward
(iii)	Workers' wages rise	inward
(iv)	New Zealand dollar appreciates resulting in a fall in the price of imported raw materials	outward
(v)	Rising oil prices	inward
(vi)	An increase in GST	inward

b Define aggregate supply.

Total production of all firms in an economy.

c Complete the following table.

	Situation	Curve/s that shifts AD and/or AS	Inward or outward
(i)	Households expect prices to rise so buy now rather than later.	AD	outward
(ii)	Households decide to increase their level of savings.	AD	inward
(iii)	Firms are confident about future sales and prospects so increase investment.	AD	outward
(iv)	Workers' productivity improves.	AS	outward
(v)	Workers' wages decrease.	AS	outward
(vi)	Direct tax cuts.	AD	outward
(vii)	Indirect tax increases.	AS	inward
(viii)	A decrease in net exports.	AD	inward
(ix)	The government runs a larger than expected budget surplus.	AD	inward
(x)	The New Zealand dollar strengthens.	AD and AS	inward outward
(xi)	Interest rates rise.	AS and AD	outward inward

d Justify your answer to **(xi)** in the table above.

(i) Aggregate supply curve.

The increase in interest rates causes the New Zealand dollar to appreciate so imported raw materials are cheaper. This lowers costs of production/increases profit so the AS shifts to the right as planned output increases.

(ii) Aggregate demand curve.

Increased interest rates decrease spending and so ↓ AD because C falls as households save more because of the higher return, or C falls because cost of borrowing higher so can't afford as much. I falls, borrowing cost higher so the profitability of future projects is reduced. Net exports fall (X ↓ – M ↑), as $NZ appreciates making M cheaper or X more expensive.

    ISBN: 9780170438131

3 a Complete the table with a tick (✓) to indicate whether the following will cause the aggregate demand curve and/or aggregate supply curve to shift.

		Shifts aggregate demand curve	Shifts aggregate supply curve
(i)	Levels of business confidence	✓	
(ii)	Changes in workers' wages		✓
(iii)	Changes in household incomes	✓	
(iv)	Costs of production		✓
(v)	Indirect tax – e.g., GST, sales tax		✓
(vi)	A tax collected by a third party and passed on to the government		✓
(vii)	Expectation about future inflation levels	✓	
(viii)	Net exports	✓	
(ix)	Changes in interest rates	✓	✓
(x)	Changes in net migration	✓	✓
(xi)	New technology and workers productivity		✓
(xii)	Changes in the value of the New Zealand dollar, e.g., depreciation	✓	✓

b List several factors that will cause the aggregate demand curve to shift outwards.

Consumption spending increases due to increased transfer payments or income (direct) tax cuts, investment spending increases due to increased business confidence or a fall in interest rates. Net migration gain. The exchange rate depreciates.

c List several factors that will cause the aggregate supply curve to shift inwards.

The costs of production rise, e.g., a wage rate increase, the cost of imported raw materials increases as a result of the New Zealand dollar depreciating. An increase in indirect taxes, or other government charges. Net migration loss. The exchange rate depreciates.

d What is aggregate supply?

Total production of all firms in the economy.

e What is aggregate demand?

Total demand in the economy. Equivalent to national income. AD = C + I + G + (X − M)

4 a Indicate if the following situations impact on aggregate demand (AD) and/or aggregate supply (AS), and in what direction (inward or outward).

	Situation	AD and/or AS	Direction of the shift
(i)	A better educated workplace.	AS	outward (right)
(ii)	Unions accept wage cuts to preserve jobs.	AS	outward (right)
(iii)	Capital expenditure by firms decreases	AD	inward (left)
(iv)	Interest rates increase	AD AS	inward (left) outward (right)
(v)	New technology improves workers' productivity	AS	outward (right)
(vi)	A government operating deficit	AD	outward (right)
(vii)	Direct tax cuts	AD	outward (right)
(viii)	Indirect tax rates are increased	AS	inward (left)
(ix)	Business confidence increases	AD	outward (right)
(x)	An increase in petrol prices	AS	inward (left)
(xi)	The New Zealand dollar appreciates	AD AS	outward (right) inward (left)
(xii)	Cheaper credit	AD	outward (right)

b Explain how a decrease in interest rates can affect aggregate demand and aggregate supply.

When interest rates decrease household consumption spending will increase because savings will decrease as households receive lower returns. Borrowing will increase because the cost of a loan will fall. Since some households pay less on mortgage repayments, their discretionary incomes will increase and therefore increase the funds they have to spend or save. These changes will cause AD to shift outward.

As interest rates fall firms are likely to increase spending on capital goods because the lower cost of borrowing will reduce the risks involved and increase the profitability of new activities. AD will shift outward.

The New Zealand dollar will depreciate when interest rates fall because this decreases demand for the New Zealand dollar and increases supply of it on the forex market. Firms that export will find that their products are more price competitive and they are able to swap forex for more $NZ. Exporters' incomes increase, causing AD to shift outward. As the New Zealand dollar depreciates the cost of imported raw materials/equipment rises. This increases the costs of production/decreases profits so the AS curve shifts inward.

5 a For each event listed below explain which direction the aggregate demand curve will shift.

(i) The Reserve Bank of New Zealand lowers interest rates.

inward (outward) (circle your choice)

Explanation: <u>When the OCR falls this will lower interest rates, this results in less savings and increased consumption spending by households and increased investment by firms, this will cause AD to increase.</u>

(ii) Inflationary expectations rise. inward (outward) (circle your choice)

Explanation: <u>Households (consumers) buy today to avoid future expected price increases, so increasing AD.</u>

(iii) The New Zealand dollar depreciates. inward (outward) (circle your choice)

Explanation: <u>A falling New Zealand dollar results in exporters swapping foreign earnings for more New Zealand dollars. The increased earnings enable more spending so cause AD to increase.</u>

(iv) Government provides additional financial support for low and middle income families.

inward (outward) (circle your choice)

Explanation: <u>Additional financial support for low and middle income families will raise their disposable income. This will increase consumption spending so AD shifts right.</u>

b (i) Identify and explain the effect of an appreciating New Zealand dollar on aggregate supply.

Effect: (Increase) Decrease (circle one)

Explanation: <u>Cheaper price for imported raw materials (which lowers the costs of production for New Zealand firms). Decreased costs increase profits, so firms plan to produce more, thereby shifting AS to the right.</u>

(ii) Explain the link between a decrease in interest rates and a shift of the AS curve.

<u>The decrease in interest rates causes the New Zealand dollar to depreciate so imported raw materials are more expensive. This raises costs of production/decreases profit so the AS shifts to the left as planned output decreases.</u>

(iii) Identify and explain the effects of unions getting a wage increase on which direction the aggregate supply curve will shift.

Identify: (inward) or outward (circle your choice)

Explanation: <u>As unions get workers a wage increase the costs of production for firms will rise. Increase costs, decrease profits so firms plan to produce less thereby AS shifts left (inward).</u>

c Explain why migration has an impact on aggregate demand and aggregate supply.

<u>Migration is a factor that impacts on aggregate demand and aggregate supply. When migrants arrive in New Zealand they will look to set up homes and are likely to buy whiteware and furniture, consumption spending will increase and aggregate demand will increase. When migrants arrive they will add to the size of the labour force and wages will fall, ceteris paribus. As wages fall, firms' costs of production will decrease. As costs of production decrease, profits will increase and aggregate supply will shift outward.</u>

6 a (i) On the axes provided, sketch and label an aggregate supply curve.

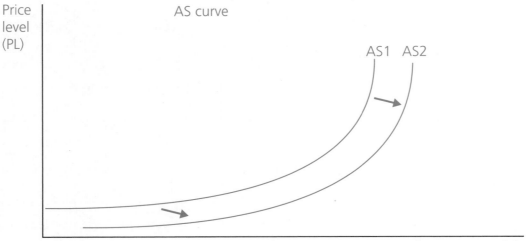

(ii) Fully label the effects of increased immigration on the AS curve.

(iii) Fully explain the change to the AS curve.

The AS curve shifts right (outward) because there is an increase in the supply of workers, so more resources are available. Costs of production to firms will fall. Costs decrease, increase in profits, so firms plan to produce more, therefore AS shifts right as shown from AS1 to AS2.

b (i) On the axes provided, sketch and label an aggregate demand curve.

(ii) Show the effect of a 'resurgent housing market' due to increased consumer confidence and spending, as house prices rise.

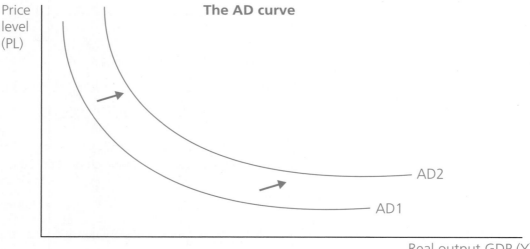

(iii) Explain why the AD curve shifted.

As consumer spending increases because house prices have increased (wealth increases) which increases consumer confidence or consumers are prepared to borrow more (or save less), this will cause AD to shift outward from AD1 to AD2.

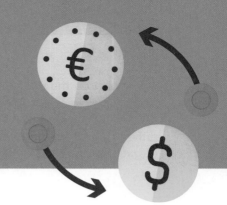

4 MACROECONOMICS
The AD/AS model

The AD/AS model

The aggregate demand (AD) and aggregate supply (AS) model is used to provide insights into the operation of an economy. It aids in understanding changes in the price level (inflation), real output GDP (economic growth), employment and unemployment.

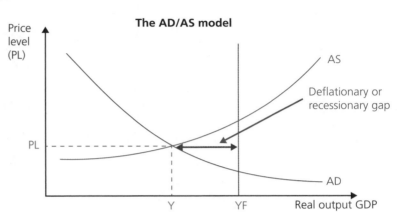

The AD/AS model

To illustrate the effects of an economic event or situation on the AD/AS model the following conventions are followed:

- the appropriate AD and/or AS curves are shifted in the appropriate direction, with a label for the new curve with arrows drawn to indicate the direction of the change.

- the new equilibrium price level is labelled PL2 (or PL') and the new equilibrium real output GDP is labelled Y2 (or Y') using dotted lines. Arrows are used to show the direction of the change in the price level and real output GDP.

An increase in the price level (or inflation) is shown on the vertical axis, with the original price level labelled PL1 (PL) and the new higher price level labelled PL2 (PL').

Changes in employment, national income and output are shown on the horizontal axis, with the original position labelled Y1 (Y) and the new position Y2 (Y'). An increase in real output GDP indicates that economic growth has taken place, i.e., an increase in actual output in the economy and an increase in employment (or decrease in unemployment).

A deflationary (or recessionary) gap shows equilibrium income is below the full employment level (YF), this is shown on the diagram above. Equilibrium real income, output and employment (Y) and the equilibrium price level (PL) is established where the AD and AS curves intersect.

An increase in output per worker (productivity) due to the use of new technology or a better educated workforce will lower costs for firms, causing the aggregate supply curve to shift outward (to the right). The price level will decrease (from PL to PL´ or PL1 to PL2) while national income, employment and output will increase (from Y to Y' or Y1 to Y2). This situation is shown in the diagram below.

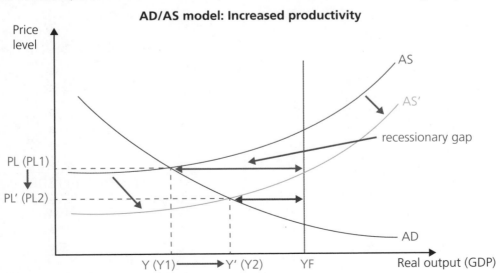

AD/AS model: Increased productivity

The impact on the AD/AS model of various shifts will differ depending on the starting position. The diagram below shows AD shifting outwards due to, for example, cuts in direct tax. On the flat section of the AS curve (at low levels of national output) there is a larger impact on output and employment rather than on the price level. On the steep or rising part of the AS curve (or closer to YF at high levels of national output) there is a larger impact on the price level than on output and employment.

AD/AS model: Starting position

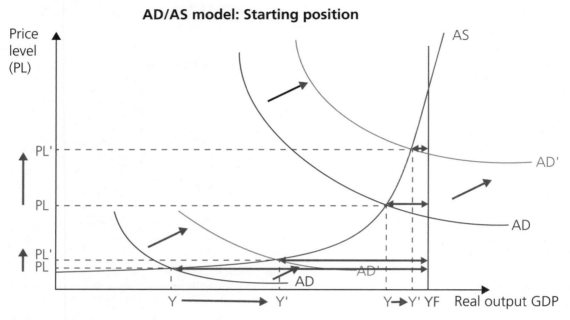

An inflationary gap

An inflationary gap is where equilibrium income is above the full employment level of income (i.e., the AD and AS curves intersect at a point beyond full employment). The situation is likely to be a temporary situation because the economy is operating at a level of output beyond its long-run capacity. For a while firms may produce the required quantity by working longer hours and paying overtime to workers. However, wages will be forced upward as firms compete for scarce labour, causing the AS curve to shift upwards to AS2. In so doing it will move the economy onto the long-run AS curve or vertical at YF (or potential real GDP), eliminating (closing) the inflationary gap.

AD/AS model: Inflationary gap

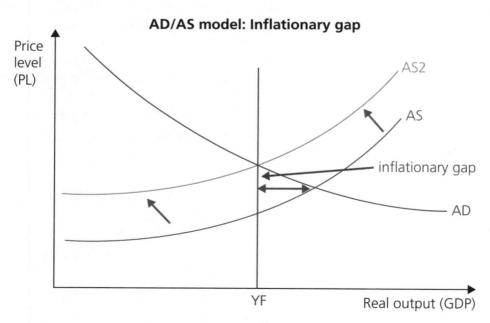

     ISBN: 9780170438131

Double shifts

When the AD and AS curves shift, the change in the general price level and real output GDP will depend on the relative size of the change in each curve. For example, a net migration gain will increase both AD and AS, they may cancel each other out with an increase in real output GDP but no change in the general price level as illustrated on the AD/AS model below. If, however, the AD shifts outward more than the increase in AS then the price level will increase.

The AD/AS model: A double shift

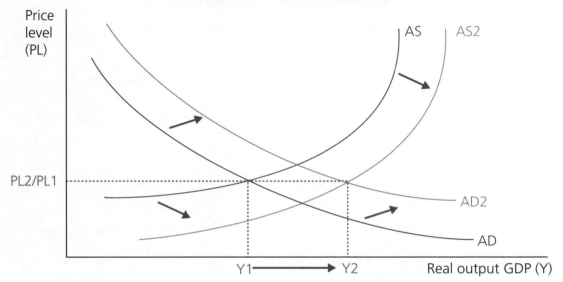

1 **a** **(i)** Show on graph one the impact of an increase in aggregate demand.

   (ii) Show on graph two the impact of a decrease in aggregate demand.

   (iii) Show on graph three the impact of an increase in aggregate supply.

   (iv) Show on graph four the impact of a decrease in aggregate supply.

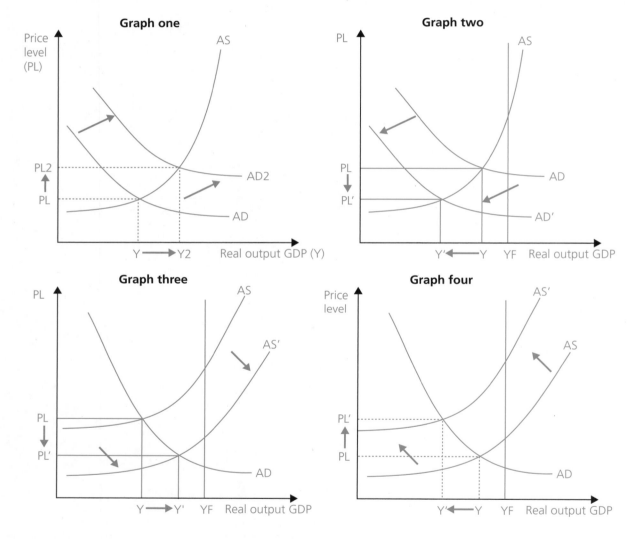

b Use the graphs above to complete the table below

Graph	Impact on the price level	Impact on employment	Impact on unemployment	Impact on economic growth
1	increase	increase	decrease	increase
2	decrease	decrease	increase	decrease
3	decrease	increase	decrease	increase
4	increase	decrease	increase	decrease

2 On each axis, carefully construct AD and AS curves to show the situation indicated by the title. Complete your diagrams by:

(i) labelling the curves and axes.

(ii) labelling the original equilibrium appropriately.

(iii) labelling the recessionary gap (↔).

(iv) labelling the changes fully.

a An improvement in technology, such as improved communications.

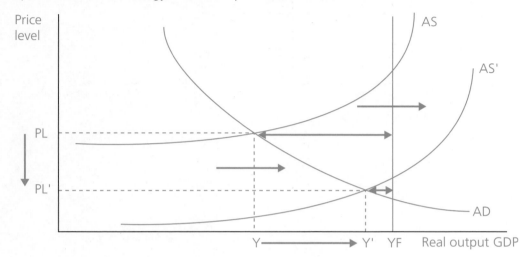

b Transport costs rise due to an increase in road user charges.

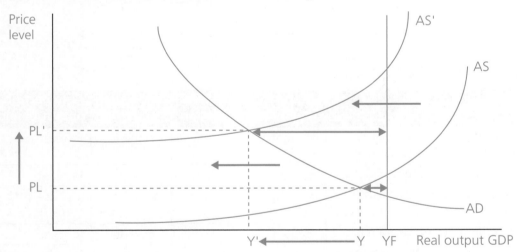

c Decreased business confidence.

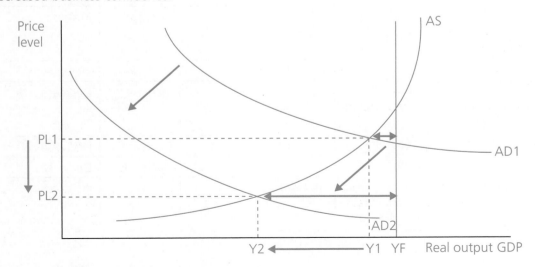

3 Draw a fully labelled diagram for the situations indicated.

a An economy with an inflationary gap.

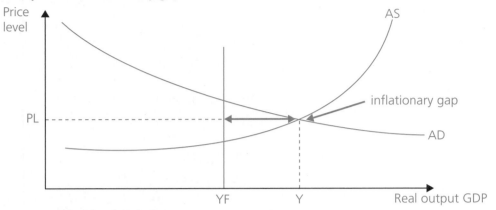

b An economy with a deflationary gap.

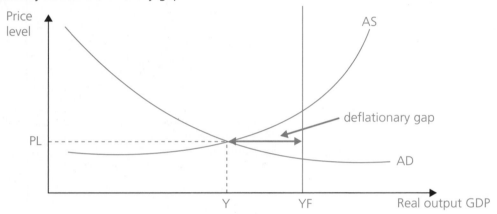

c Complete the table below for shifts in the AD or AS curve.

	Situation	AD or AS curve shifts and in what direction	Impact on PL	Impact on real output/employment
(i)	Cost of imported raw materials decreases due to $NZ appreciating	AS right	Decrease	Increase
(ii)	Productivity of workers improves	AS right	Decrease	Increase
(iii)	Workers accept a lower wage award to keep jobs	AS right	Decrease	Increase
(iv)	Fall in the cost of raw materials.	AS right	Decrease	Increase
(v)	Recession in New Zealand's major trading partners	AD left	Decrease	Decrease
(vi)	Renewed confidence in the economy by New Zealand business people	AD right	Increase	Increase
(vii)	A cut in direct tax rate	AD right	Increase	Increase
(viii)	The cost of raw materials has increased due to the New Zealand dollar depreciating	AS left	Increase	Decrease
(ix)	A government budget surplus	AD left	Decrease	Decrease
(x)	Decreased transfer payments	AD left	Decrease	Decrease
(xi)	The Minister of Finance announces that GST will increase by 1.5% in ten months time	AD right	Increase	Increase

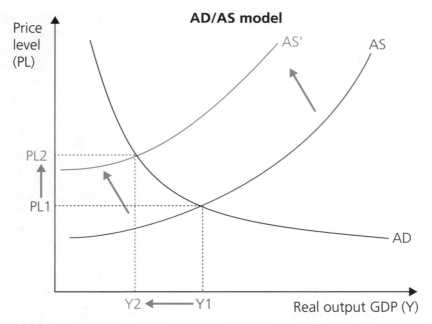

AD/AS model

4 **a (i)** Show on the diagram above the effect of an increase in the cost of imported raw materials. Label fully.

(ii) Explain the change you have shown in **a (i)** above.

The increase in the cost of imported raw materials causes firms' costs of production to increase causing aggregate supply to shift inward. This will cause cost-push inflation as shown by the increase from PL1 to PL2.

b For each event in the table below, describe its likely impact on the AD/AS model by ticking the appropriate column.

Event	AD		AS		Price level		Real GDP	
	Increase	Decrease	Increase	Decrease	Increase	Decrease	Increase	Decrease
(i) Increased business confidence	✓				✓		✓	
(ii) Wages increase				✓	✓			✓
(iii) A fall in productivity				✓	✓			✓
(iv) A government budget deficit	✓				✓		✓	
(v) High prices for dairy exports	✓				✓		✓	
(vi) Decrease in direct taxes	✓				✓		✓	
(vii) Increase in GST				✓	✓			✓
(viii) Cost of imported raw materials falls			✓			✓	✓	

5 Discuss the idea that 'The relative impact on the price level and output will differ depending on the original equilibrium position on the AD/AS model'. Draw an AD/AS model to support your answer.

AD/AS model: Starting position

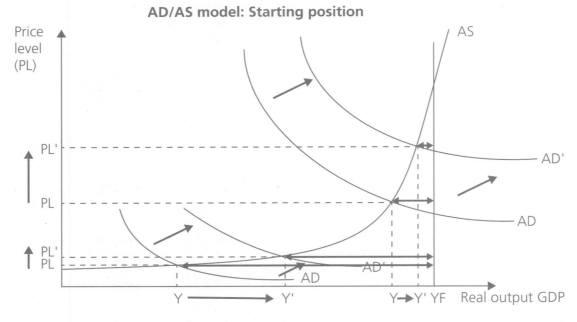

At low levels of national output (the flat part of AS) there is a considerable effect on output and employment with little impact on the price level, as there is probably idle capacity and unemployed workers. At higher levels of national output (the rising part of AS, closer to YF) there will be a large impact on the price level compared to output and employment. Resources that were idle are now employed and firms will need to bid scarce resources away from other industries, or pay overtime to get extra output. Costs of production will rise significantly.

PHOTOCOPYING OF THIS PAGE IS RESTRICTED UNDER LAW.   ISBN: 9780170438131

6 Explain the effects of a net migration gain on the economy.

In your answer you should:

- Draw and fully label an AD/AS model to show the effect of migration changes.
- Explain the changes to the AD and AS curves.
- Explain how a net migration gain has impact on inflation and growth.

AD/AS model showing net migration gain

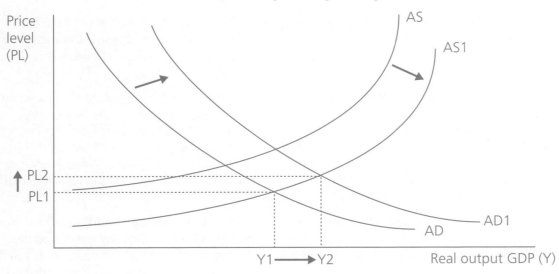

When new migrants arrive in a country they will look to set up house and buy whiteware (appliances) and other household effects. They will also buy or build houses. Aggregate demand will therefore shift outward. The AS curve shifts right (outward) because there is an increase in the supply of workers, so more resources are available. Costs of production to firms will fall. Costs decrease, profits increase, so firms plan to produce more, therefore AS shifts right.

The AD and AS curves have both shifted outward (to the right), and this has resulted in an increase in real output GDP which is economic growth, shown as the change from Y1 to Y2. It has also resulted in an increase in the general price level shown as the change from PL1 to PL2, which is inflation.

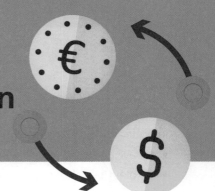

Household income (Y)

A household is either a person or a group of people living under one roof. A household's income (Y) comes from supplying labour (human) resources to firms in return for wages. **Disposable income** is income after direct (income) taxes are paid and any transfers received. When direct (income) tax rates are cut or transfers increase then disposable incomes rise.

A household's **discretionary income** is a household's disposable income minus all essential payments required. Essential payments would include items such as mortgage repayments, insurance, rates, groceries, utilities such as power and water, and other necessities. What is left over from a household's disposable income after other commitments are accounted for is a household's discretionary income. The remaining income can either be used for additional spending or can be saved. When interest rates paid on a variable mortgage fall then a household will pay less for its mortgage, this will result in an increase in discretionary income rather than disposable income.

A household can either spend or save the income they receive. **Consumption spending (C)** is household spending (or expenditure) on goods and services and is likely to increase when incomes rise. **Savings (S)** represents income not spent. The level of savings a household has will depend on several factors including interest rates, expectations about the future and attitudes towards thrift. Individuals may save more if they are concerned about the future and desire to have funds for an emergency, such as an unexpected bill for repairs to a house or car. As interest rates increase individuals are likely to save more because they are receiving a higher return on funds put aside to use later.

Consumption spending (C)

Consumption spending (C) is a component of Aggregate Demand (AD). As consumption spending increases the aggregate demand curve will shift outward (to the right) causing an increase in real output GDP (growth) and an increase in the price level (inflation), ceteris paribus.

Consumption spending (C) will increase if:

- **Household disposable incomes (HDI) increase**. When household disposable incomes increase they can afford more. Household disposable incomes will increase if direct (income) taxes are cut and/or transfer payments are increased.

- **Interest rates fall**. If interest rates fall there is less incentive for households to save because they get a lower return. This will discourage savings and therefore consumption spending will increase. If interest rates fall then it is possible that households will get a loan to buy items they desire (whiteware, cars, furniture) or to do renovations to homes or buy a property (home), this will increase consumption spending.

  When interest rates fall, there may be little or no change in consumption spending because if there are a significant number of households with fixed (interest rate) mortgages then a fall in interest rates will not make any difference to the repayments they make. As their discretionary income remains unchanged, it is likely that consumption spending will also remain unchanged.

- **Inflationary expectations increase**. If households are concerned that the general price level is going to increase, then they will buy now, rather than later when goods and services are more expensive. This will cause consumption spending to increase.

- **Wealth effect**. If property and house prices increase then households may be encouraged to borrow more from banks and financial institutions by asking for a loan based on the increased equity they have in their home and/or property. As borrowed funds are spent on goods and services consumption spending (C) increases.

ISBN: 9780170438131

A change in **households' attitudes** can influence consumption spending, for example, households may decide to reduce levels of debt. An increase in income that arises from direct tax may see little change in consumption spending because the additional disposable income households receive is used to pay back loans.

Consumer confidence can influence the level of consumption spending. If households are more concerned about the future they may decide to save more and reduce consumption spending. As more households participate in (or join) savings schemes (e.g., Kiwisaver) and/or increase their contributions then consumption spending (C) will decrease, causing aggregate demand to decrease.

Consumption spending (C) will impact on firms because as households demand more goods and services, firms will need to increase production. As a part of increasing production firms will need to use additional resources and employ more workers or pay existing workers overtime. Therefore household incomes will rise and additional consumption spending will occur. Firms will collect more indirect tax from the increased spending on goods and services by households. As firms' incomes increase from increased sales it is likely that profits will increase, as profits increase firms will pay direct (company) tax to the government. Overall the prospects of profits in the future may lead to an increase in business confidence, with firms deciding to expand their operations and subsequently buy new capital goods (invest) to increase output.

1 **a** Explain the difference between disposable income and discretionary income.

Disposable income is income after direct (income) taxes are paid and any transfers received. A household's discretionary income is a household's disposable income minus all essential payments required.

b Explain the different effect that an increase in direct tax and an increase in interest rates will have on a household's disposable income and/or discretionary income and their level of consumption spending.

An increase in direct tax will decrease a household's disposable income. A decrease in disposable income will result in a decrease in consumption spending because households can not afford as much.

An increase in interest rates will increase the reward for savings, so savings will increase and consumption spending will fall. As interest rates increase this will increase the cost of borrowing, therefore households will be less likely to increase debt to finance their spending. When interest rates paid on a variable mortgage increase then a household will pay more for its mortgage, this will result in a decrease in discretionary income rather than disposable income.

c Define savings.

Savings (S) represents income not spent.

d Outline several factors that determine household savings.

The level of savings a household has will depend on several factors including interest rates, expectations about the future and attitudes towards thrift. Individuals may save more if they are concerned about the future and desire to have funds for an emergency, such as an unexpected bill for repairs to a house or car. As interest rates increase individuals are likely to save more because they are receiving a higher return on funds put aside to use later.

2 **a** State factors that can influence consumption spending.

<u>Disposable income, direct taxes, transfer payments, expectations about the future, interest rates, wealth</u>

<u>effect, attitudes towards debt level, attitude towards savings.</u>

b Explain in detail the likely effect of an increase in interest rates on consumption expenditure.

<u>As interest rates increase it is likely that households will save more because they are receiving a higher</u>

<u>return on funds put aside, therefore consumption spending will fall. As interest rates increase households</u>

<u>will pay more on mortgages and credit cards, discretionary income will fall. Households are likely to take</u>

<u>out fewer loans because the cost of borrowing has increased and this will cause consumption spending</u>

<u>to fall.</u>

c Compare and contrast the effect of a decrease in direct taxes and an increase in transfer payments.

<u>A decrease in direct taxes and increase in transfer payments will both increase households' disposable</u>

<u>incomes and increase consumption spending.</u>

<u>A decrease in direct taxes is likely to have a greater effect on consumption spending than an increase</u>

<u>in transfer payments because more households earn an income than those that receive a benefit.</u>

> Inflationary expectations will influence household behaviour.

d **(i)** Explain the impact of lower inflationary expectations on household consumption.

   (ii) Explain the impact of lower inflationary expectations on the level of borrowing by households and household debt.

<u>Lower inflationary expectations will reduce household consumption spending because it will curb</u>

<u>the desire to spend and borrow. Consumption spending by households is likely to fall because there</u>

<u>will be less need for spending to take place before prices increase when inflationary expectations</u>

<u>are low. When consumption spending falls household savings will increase.</u>

<u>Lower inflation rates mean that the real value of any interest paid on debt is increased, making</u>

<u>debt less desirable, therefore households will pay down debt and borrow less. Benefits or gains</u>

<u>that might have been achieved through the repayment of debt by the falling real value of the sum</u>

<u>of the loans borrowed will decline.</u>

3 Explain the effect of changes in consumption spending on inflation.

In your answer you should:

- Explain the effect on wealth of increasing house prices.
- Explain the effect of cuts in direct taxes.
- Explain the effect of increased immigration.
- Draw a model to support your answer.

As house prices increase, households will feel more wealthy as the equity in their houses increases. This will result in some households increasing the level of borrowing against the increased value of their homes to buy or consume other goods and services. As spending increases AD will shift outward, causing demand-pull inflation as the general price level increases.

Cuts in direct (income) tax will increase household disposable income and consumption spending will increase. As spending increases AD will shift outward, causing demand-pull inflation as the general price level increases.

When new migrants arrive in a country they will look to set up house and buy whiteware (appliances) and other household effects. They will also buy or build houses. Aggregate demand will therefore shift outward as a result of this increased consumption spending, causing demand-pull inflation as the general price level increases.

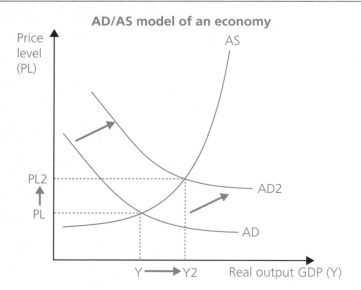

AD/AS model of an economy

There will be an increase in the price level (inflation) as indicated by the change from PL to PL2 and real output GDP, i.e., growth, as indicated by the change from Y to Y2.

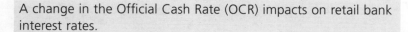

A change in the Official Cash Rate (OCR) impacts on retail bank interest rates.

4 **a** Explain the impact of a decrease in interest rates on economic activity.

In your answer you should:
- Explain the effect of a decrease in interest rates on consumers.
- Explain the effect of a decrease in interest rates on producers.
- Explain why the changes may not be as significant as you predict.

As the OCR decreases interest rates would fall. Household consumption spending would increase because savings would decrease as households receive lower returns. Borrowing would increase because the cost of a loan would fall. As some households pay less on mortgage repayments, their discretionary incomes would increase and increase the funds they have to spend or save. These changes will cause AD to shift outward.

As interest rates fall firms are likely to increase spending on capital goods because the lower cost of borrowing will reduce the risks involved and increase the profitability of new activites. AD will shift outward. The decrease in interest rates is likely to cause the dollar to depreciate. Firms that export will find that their products are more price competitive and they are able to swap forex for more $NZ. Incomes of exporters increase, causing AD to shift outward.

The changes in consumer and producer responses to a decrease in interest rates may not be as significant as I predicted because there will be a 'time lag', i.e., there will be a delay of time between the announcement of a change to the OCR and the effect on interest rates that apply to households and firms. Also, when interest rates fall, some households and firms have fixed mortgages so the change in the OCR has no effect on them. Firms will not necessarily invest more as interest rates fall because they may not be confident about the future and unwilling to take the risk of investing despite the cheaper loans available.

b State, for each situation, which event or situation will have a larger impact on economic activity and explain why.

(i) A decrease in interest rates or an increase in house prices.

A decrease in interest rates will have a larger impact on economic activity because it will impact on consumption spending, investment spending and net exports. An increase in house prices only impacts on consumption spending if households take out loans against the increased equity of their houses and increase spending.

(ii) A decrease in transfer payments or an increase in direct taxes.

An increase in direct taxes will have a greater impact on economic activity because most households earn an income while there are fewer people on a benefit (transfer payments).

MACROECONOMICS
Firms and investment spending (I)

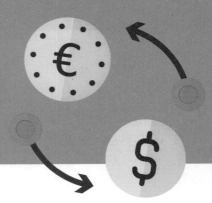

Investment (I)

Investment spending (I) or capital formation takes place when firms buy capital. For example, a farmer buys a quad bike, a horticulturist builds a dam for irrigation purposes or a manufacturer installs new machinery. Investment spending (I) is a component of aggregate demand (AD).

Businesses are more likely to increase their level of investment spending (capital expenditure) if they are confident about the prospects of a venture or project being successful. As part of this process of deciding to invest (purchase new capital items) or not, firms will consider the cost of borrowing the funds required (i.e., interest rates), the level of risk involved as well as the profitability of the decision.

Before investment funds are available to firms, those funds need to be saved by households with financial institutions, this enables financial institutions to have funds available to advance (lend) to firms who want to buy capital. When interest rates fall investment should increase, however this is not always the case. Financial institutions may be unable to find credit worthy firms to make advances to, or firms may not wish to invest despite lower interest rates because they are not confident about the future or simply have little or no desire to expand because they have a goal of satisficing. Satisficing is a business goal of being content with a certain profit or sales target rather than maximising profit or sales.

As interest rates increase then firms are less likely to invest because the risk is higher and the profitability is reduced because the cost of borrowing funds has increased. Investment spending will fall and decrease aggregate demand.

If interest rates fall or are lower, then spending on a new factory or a piece of equipment is more likely because the cost of borrowing is lower and the associated risks reduced, which make the project likely to be more profitable.

There exists a link between investment spending and the balance of payments on the current account because some capital items have to be purchased from overseas suppliers if New Zealand does not produce these items (machinery, equipment, tools). As imports of capital goods from overseas rise it will increase the current account deficit or make a current account surplus smaller.

A stable exchange rate will make business decisions more predictable because firms will be more assured about their costs and incomes. This is likely to increase business confidence in future profits and increase their willingness to buy capital goods (investment). Greater investment will result in an increase in aggregate demand and an increase both in real output GDP (economic growth) and the general price level (inflation).

Inflation and firms

Investment can only take place if there is savings. Inflation encourages spending and discourages savings, so funds that might otherwise have been available for investment tend to dry up.

In periods of high inflation investment tends to get discouraged because of uncertainty over future revenues, costs and profitability of business ventures. Planning and investment decisions become more difficult to predict because firms are unsure what will happen to prices and costs during times of inflation. Not all firms pass on the increases in costs in the form of price increases because some will absorb these costs because their markets are price sensitive and a price increase could result in falling sales. If firms are unable to pass on the increase in costs to consumers this will have an impact on profits, possibly causing some firms to close or cut back production and subsequent employment. With lower levels of investment there is likely to be a slowing of the rate of growth of national output (GDP). This in turn leads to a reduction in new jobs and so can increase the level of unemployment.

     ISBN: 9780170438131

A firm's costs can remain unchanged despite inflation taking place because they have signed contracts that keep input costs stable. Some firms will be confident about the future so investment will increase despite inflation taking place, more so if the rate of inflation is low.

Price changes act as signals directing economic activity. Increasing prices indicate excess demand (a shortage) and will stimulate production, while falling prices will direct producers to produce less or to shift into new activities. Inflation can distort market price signals and the market may fail to allocate resources efficiently.

Low levels of inflation are likely to mean lower interest rates in an economy. Lower interest rates mean that firms will be more inclined to invest (purchase capital goods) because the cost of borrowing has decreased, reducing the risk of failure because ventures are likely to be more profitable. As investment spending increases, aggregate demand (AD) shifts outward causing the general price level to increase (demand-pull inflation) and an increase in real output GDP, which is economic growth. Low levels of inflation mean that firms are able to plan with more confidence because costs and prices are more certain. Also, domestic producers will be more able to compete with cheaper imported products because low inflation means that their products remain price competitive.

In times of inflation trade unions will seek to obtain higher wages for union members. If trade unions are able to negotiate higher wages this will increase the costs of production for firms, without increasing firms' revenue or incomes. Firms will seek to recover the higher costs they now face by increasing their prices in an effort to maintain their profits. The increase in prices represents inflation. In response to higher costs and prices firms may reduce output because higher prices will result in a decrease in quantity demanded by consumers. As firms reduce output they need fewer resources (labour) and employment could decrease as a result.

Firms, inflation and trade

The rate of inflation impacts on exports (X) and imports (M). When inflation in a country is at a higher rate than its trading partners it can lead to increased demand for imports, because they become relatively cheaper. At the same time, the competiveness of exports will decrease because the costs of production in the economy are assumed to be rising faster than those of overseas competitors' exports, then exports are likely to decrease. Ultimately this can lead to a deterioration in the balance of payments on the current account (a greater deficit or smaller surplus) because import payments increase and export receipts fall.

Generally, high rates of inflation can harm exporters because their goods and services are less price competitive and therefore more difficult to sell. Importers can benefit from high rates of inflation because their goods and services are relatively more price competitive than those produced or provided by local (domestic) firms.

However, if inflation rates are low, exporters are likely to benefit and importers lose. One benefit of low inflation for a country is that exports will be relatively more price competitive, while imports from trading partners will be relatively more expensive. This is likely to result in export-led growth in the economy because aggregate demand will increase. The main benefit of consistent lower inflation for firms will be that stable prices provides greater certainty about current and future projects and that lowers the risks involved in running a business. It will also encourage firms to invest because business confidence increases, this is conducive to long-term growth.

1 a In economics what is meant by the term investment and who will undertake it?

Investment spending (I) or capital formation takes place when firms buy capital.

b In what circumstances is investment likely to increase?

Investment is likely to increase when firms are confident about new business ventures. When interest rates fall firms are more likely to invest because the risk is lower and the profitability of new ventures increased because the cost of borrowing funds has decreased.

c When interest rates fall investment should increase. Explain why this is not always the case.

Investment may not take place when interest rates fall because firms are not confident about the future and perceive the risks to be higher and the profitability of ventures as being lower. Some firms may be content will the status quo and not desire to expand the size of their business and/or market. Banks may find they are unable to find credit worthy firms to make advances to, despite interest rates falling.

d Explain the possible link between an increase in investment spending and the current account balance.

Investment spending involves the buying of capital goods, some of which will need to be imported from overseas. This will cause import payments in the balance of goods to increase. As import payments increase the current account deficit could increase or a current account surplus become smaller.

Farmers are looking at increased capital
expenditure on irrigation projects

2 a Explain the effects of increased capital expenditure on irrigation projects.
In your answer you should:

- Show the effects on the AD/AS model.
- Explain the effect on economic growth, inflation and employment.
- Refer to your diagram.

AD/AS model of an economy

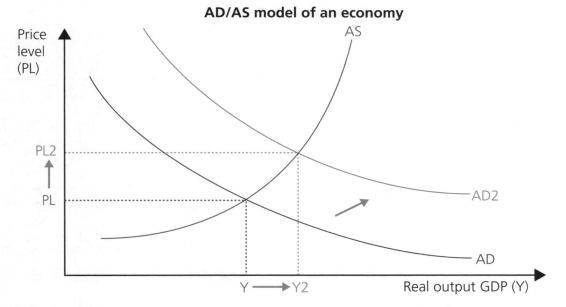

The increased investment (capital expenditure) by farmers on irrigation projects will increase economic
growth (shown as the increase in real output GDP from Y to Y2) because the aggregate demand curve
shifts outward/right from AD to AD2.

There will be an increase in the general price level (inflation), illustrated by the increase from PL to PL2.
As real output increases firms will be looking to satisfy demand so they will employ additional workers,
shown as the increase from Y to Y2. Therefore, employment will increase and unemployment will
decrease.

b Complete the table.

Event	Likely impact on investment
(i) Business confidence increases.	increase
(ii) An upswing in the business cycle.	increase
(iii) A recession.	decrease
(iv) A major sporting event is to start in several years' time.	increase
(v) Interest rates increase.	decrease

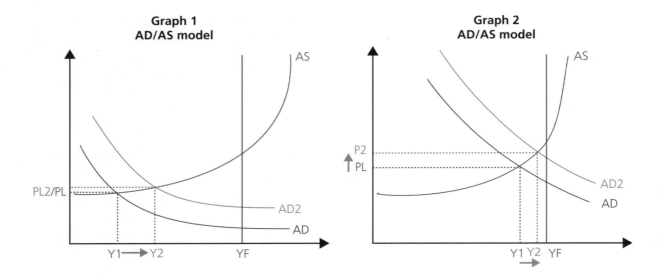

Graph 1
AD/AS model

Graph 2
AD/AS model

3 a (i) Illustrate the impact on the economy of increased business confidence on both diagrams above. Label the changes fully.

(ii) Explain in detail the changes made on both diagrams, and the impact of these changes on the goal of price stability of keeping inflation between 1% and 3% on average over the medium term (Policy Target Agreement). Outline how the government might react.

An increase in business confidence will result in an increase in investment spending by firms, shown by the AD curve shifting outward from AD to AD2 on both diagrams.

On Graph 1 the economy is operating at a low level of national output, the increase in investment has a small impact on the price level (PL to PL2) with a larger impact on output (Y to Y2). There will be less inflationary pressure in the economy in this instance with the change in the lower end of the policty target agrement. The government may react and lower interest rates to stimulate economic activity or pursue an expansionary fiscal policy.

On Graph 2 the economy is operating at a high level of national output (income), close to full employment. The increase in investment has a relatively small impact on national output with a larger increase in the price level. The government may react to the inflationary pressures in the economy (shown by the increase of PL to PL2) by increasing interest rates to dampen economic activity, or pursue a contractionary fiscal policy.

4 a Explain how an increase in the rate of inflation would impact on overseas trade.

Exports relatively more expensive to overseas buyers so export receipts might fall; our exports are less competitive for our trading partners. Imports are cheaper relative to New Zealand goods so import payments rise; locally produced goods are less competitive to imports so import payments will increase.

b Outline the negative impact of inflation on firms.

Rising costs (includes increase in wages, raw materials, interest rates); difficult to replace old equipment; planning difficulties; exports become relatively less competitive; speculative rather than productive investment is encouraged; less investment.

c To reduce inflation interest rates may rise and the New Zealand dollar appreciates. Justify the government position for keeping prices stable from a trade perspective.

One benefit of low inflation is that if New Zealand's inflation rate is below that of our trading partners, then New Zealand exports will be relatively more price competitive, therefore exports will increase (imports to New Zealand will be relatively more expensive), so more export-led growth/demand for New Zealand goods. Therefore, the long-term gains of low inflation will outweigh the short-term costs due to high interest/exchange rates. The main benefit of lower inflation is a stable economy, which allows firms/households to plan with greater certainty/firms more likely to expand/invest/better price signals, which will lead to long-term growth. Therefore the (long-term) gains will outweigh the (short-term) costs due to high interest/exchange rates (such as less demand for goods and services/less growth, etc).

5 a Explain why high inflation may discourage investment and the impact this can have on economic growth and unemployment.

In periods of high inflation investment tends to get discouraged because of uncertainty over future revenues, costs and profitability of business ventures. Planning and investment decisions become more difficult to predict because firms are unsure what will happen to prices and costs during times of inflation. Not all firms pass on the increases in costs in the form of price increases because some will absorb these costs because their markets are price sensitive and a price increase could result in falling sales. If firms are unable to pass on the increase in costs to consumers this will have an impact on profits, possibly causing some firms to close or cut back production and subsequent employment. With lower levels of investment there is likely to be a slowing of the rate of growth of national output (GDP). This in turn leads to a reduction in new jobs and so can increase the level of unemployment.

b Explain the link between rates of inflation and trade.

The rate of inflation impacts on exports (X) and imports (M). When inflation in a country is at a higher rate than its trading partners it can lead to increased demand for imports, because they become relatively cheaper. At the same time, if the competiveness of exports will decrease because the costs of production in the economy are assumed to be rising faster than those of competitors' exports, then exports are likely to decrease. Ultimately this can lead to a deterioration in the balance of payments on the current account (a greater deficit or smaller surplus) because import payments increase and export receipts fall.

Generally, high rates of inflation can harm exporters because their goods and services are less price competitive and therefore more difficult to sell. Importers can benefit from high rates of inflation because their goods and services are relatively more price competitive than those produced or provided by local (domestic) firms.

However, if inflation rates are low, exporters are likely to benefit and importers lose. One benefit of low inflation for a country is that exports will be relatively more price competitive, while imports from trading partners will be relatively more expensive. This is likely to result in export-led growth in the economy because aggregate demand will increase. The main benefit of consistent lower inflation for firms will be that stable prices provides greater certainty about current and future projects and that lowers the risks involved in running a business. It will also encourage firms to invest because business confidence increases, this is conducive to long-term growth.

    ISBN: 9780170438131

6 a (i) Show the change on each AD/AS model indicated by the title.

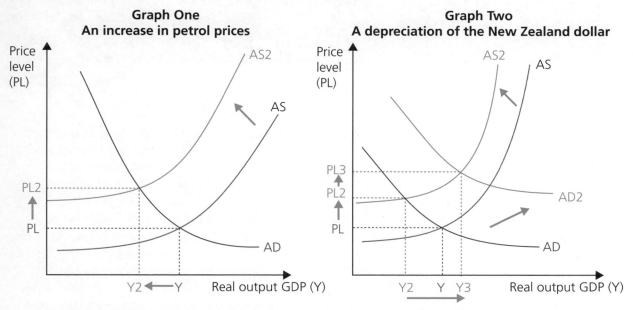

**Graph One
An increase in petrol prices**

Price level (PL) · AS2 · AS · PL2 · PL · AD · Y2 ← Y · Real output GDP (Y)

**Graph Two
A depreciation of the New Zealand dollar**

Price level (PL) · AS2 · AS · PL3 · PL2 · PL · AD2 · AD · Y2 · Y · Y3 · Real output GDP (Y)

(ii) Compare and contrast the effects on inflation of an increase in petrol prices and a depreciation of the New Zealand dollar. In your answer you should refer to the diagrams.

- Explain in detail the changes made on both graphs.

- Explain in detail why the depreciation of the New Zealand dollar may have a greater effect on inflation than an increase in petrol prices.

An increase in petrol costs will affect the transport costs of firms. As costs of production increase, profits will decrease. The AS curve will shift inward, causing the general price level to increase (as shown on Graph One as PL to PL2) as firms increase prices to maintain profits.

A depreciation of the New Zealand dollar would mean that New Zealand exports would become more price competitive and exporters would swap forex for more New Zealand dollars. AD would shift outward from AD to AD2 on Graph Two as exporters' incomes increase. A depreciation of the New Zealand dollar would increase the cost of imports. As costs increase, profits decrease and the AS curve will shift inward (from AS to AS2 on Graph Two) causing inflation. The overall increase in the price level is from PL to PL3.

Both events cause inflation (shown on both diagrams as the increase in the price level). The depreciation of the New Zealand dollar would have a greater effect on inflation than an increase in petrol prices because it impacts on both AS and AD. The increase in AD caused by the depreciation of the New Zealand dollar causes a further increase in the price level (PL) on Graph Two to PL3 as shown.

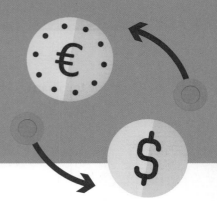

Economic activity

The **business cycle** (sometimes called the trade cycle) describes the recurring fluctuations in economic activity experienced by most economies. These fluctuations in economic activity typically follow four phases – expansion, peak, contraction and trough, as shown in the wavelike motion of the graph. These phases can vary in intensity and the length of time over which they occur. The level of economic activity in an economy is likely to vary continuously because economic conditions change on an irregular basis – e.g., levels of business confidence, consumer spending patterns and world events.

A **peak (boom)** in the trade cycle occurs when the economy is experiencing high rates of growth with the likelihood of inflationary pressures. In the boom phase there will be increased consumption spending as household incomes increase, high business confidence with increased investment and increasing government tax receipts. During a peak in the business cycle there is likely to be a decrease in the unemployment rate as firms hire additional workers to increase output. The government is likely to dampen economic activity by increasing interest rates, increasing taxes and decreasing government expenditure and have an operating (budget) surplus.

Real output (Q) may be relatively constant at the top end of the business cycle because the economy is near full capacity (i.e., the peak), resources are almost fully employed and real output (Q) has little or no room to expand any further.

A **recession** is said to occur if an economy experiences two or more consecutive quarters of negative growth (i.e., a fall in Real GDP). A hard landing in the business cycle is when an economy moves from growth to experiencing negative growth (a recession). A soft landing in the business cycle is where an economy moves from growth to slow growth, but avoids a recession.

In the recession/depression phase of the business cycle it is likely there will be high unemployment, reduced consumption spending and more business failures. This will have a flow on effect to investment where business confidence will be low. Firms are also likely to lay off staff due to the lack of demand. This will heighten levels of unemployment further, possibly causing a further downturn. Inflationary pressures are likely to be low because the economy has idle or spare capacity and firms will not need to bid scarce resources away from other industries. The government is likely to stimulate economic activity by lowering interest rates, lowering taxes and increasing government expenditure and have an operating (budget) deficit.

The **depression** phase is characterised by significant numbers of unemployed, very low levels of business confidence and a slowing of price rises. Economies, sooner or later, emerge from a recession into a period of economic growth. This early stage of an economic expansion is termed an upswing or recovery. An upswing or recovery will result in greater business confidence and investment in the economy with the likelihood of greater employment opportunities.

The business cycle

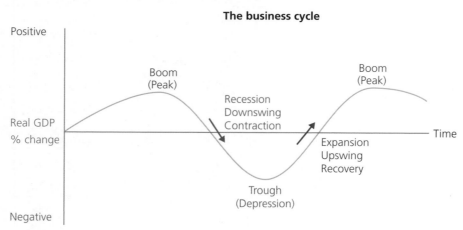

Government spending

Government spending (G) is a component of aggregate demand.

In times of a boom there is more economic activity, more goods and services are produced and unemployment decreases. The government will collect more in direct tax because there are more people employed, also the government will collect more in indirect tax from firms because household spending increases due to higher incomes. The government will pay less in transfer payments because unemployment decreases. Overall increased tax revenues and decreased government spending will increase the operating balance, resulting in a greater surplus or smaller deficit.

Fiscal policy is where government controls the level of economic activity by changing its own spending and income. The level of government activity will depend on the state of the economy. If the level of economic activity is near capacity and there is inflationary pressure, then the government will run a budget surplus (contractionary fiscal policy) to dampen down the level of economic activity. This contractionary fiscal policy will involve an increase in taxes and/or a decrease in government spending causing aggregate demand to decrease. The price level will decrease and real output GDP will fall.

The AD/AS model illustrating an operating (budget) surplus (contractionary fiscal policy)

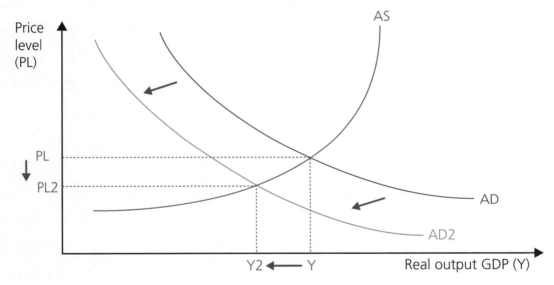

QUESTIONS & TASKS

Government operating balances ($m)		
Year 1	Year 2	Year 3
$8 000 deficit	$4 500 deficit	$1 500 deficit

1 **a** Discuss the effect of an operating deficit on the economy.
  - Describe how the operating balance is calculated.
  - Explain a fiscal policy the government could use in times of a recession to stimulate growth.
  - Explain the link between a recession and the operating balance.

The operating balance is calculated by taking government revenue (income) away from the government expenses (spending).

To stimulate economic growth the government should implement an expansionary fiscal policy by running a budget (operating) deficit. This will involve increasing government spending and/or decreasing taxes. For example if the government cuts direct taxes households' disposable incomes increase and consumption spending will increase. This will increase aggregate demand and stimulate economic activity.

In times of a recession there is less economic activity and unemployment will increase. The government will collect less in direct tax because there are fewer people employed, also the government will collect less in indirect tax from firms because household spending will fall due to lower incomes. The government will pay more in transfer payments as unemployment increases. Also because students stay longer in education or delay leaving school then education spending will increase. Overall decreased tax revenues and increased government spending will decrease the operating balance, resulting in a smaller surplus or greater deficit.

b Draw an AD/AS model to show the effects of a government operating deficit.

AD/AS model: An operating deficit

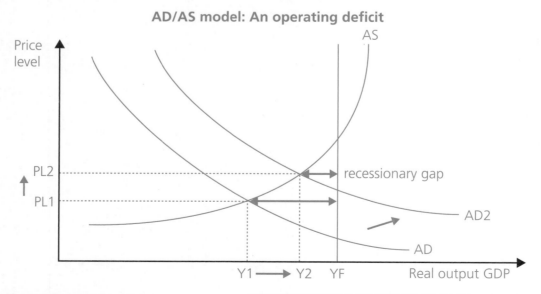

PHOTOCOPYING OF THIS PAGE IS RESTRICTED UNDER LAW.   ISBN: 9780170438131

2 **a** Explain how a boom in the global economy will impact on households, firms and the government.

As an economy experiences a boom or an increase in the level of economic activity, firms will find that stock (inventory) levels fall as sales increase. This will cause firms to increase output and employ more workers and resources. As employment rises household incomes will increase and consumption spending will rise. Business confidence is likely to rise resulting in an increase in investment spending because firms view the risks of starting a new venture or purchasing capital as being lower and more profitable. A rise in consumption spending and investment will cause aggregate demand to increase causing an increase in inflationary pressures and an increase in real output GDP.

During a boom the government will collect more in direct tax because more workers are hired (employed) because firms hire staff or pay more overtime to existing workers to cover increased output. Business profits rise with greater sales and revenue. Firms pay more company tax to the government. Government spending on transfer payments will decrease because fewer people receive a benefit. The government will collect more in indirect tax, such as GST because household consumption spending increases.

b Explain the impact on government tax revenue during a recession

During a recession the government will collect less in direct tax because fewer workers are hired (employed) and firms lay off staff or pay less overtime to workers because of reduced output. Business profits decline with fewer sales and revenue. Firms will pay less company tax to the government. Government spending on transfer payments will increase because newly unemployed workers now receive a benefit. The government will collect less in indirect tax, such as GST because household consumption spending falls.

New Zealand is part of the global economy with our trading patterns determined, in part, by events sometimes beyond the government's control. For each event outlined below, explain if the outcome for New Zealand is likely to be positive or negative.

3 a Event: A major outbreak of foot and mouth disease in Europe.

Positive effect for New Zealand, increased demand for New Zealand mutton, lamb and beef. Increased production, economic growth, greater employment and incomes for these industries and associated industries or communities. Greater export receipts will improve New Zealand's balance of payments.

b Event: A major earthquake in Auckland destroys the port and infrastructure of the city.

Negative effect for New Zealand, exports will be held up or shipments destroyed. Overseas buyers unable to access New Zealand goods will turn to other overseas suppliers for goods they require. Lost export markets may never be recovered. There will be a resulting downturn in economic activity, unemployment and low or no growth.

c Event: New Zealand misses out on signing up to a new trade agreement between many Asian countries.

Negative effect for New Zealand because it could disrupt trade. It may make it more difficult for New Zealand goods to gain access to markets in these countries. There will be a flow-on effect with less production, slower or no economic growth, a possible rise in unemployment if markets are lost or firm's expansion plans are put on hold.

       ISBN: 9780170438131

4 Study the table and answer the questions that follow.

Year	Percentage change in Real GDP
1	2.8
2	0.5
3	−1.4
4	2.9
5	5.1

a (i) What happened in Year 4 and Year 5?

The economy grew (possibly experiencing a boom in the trade
cycle).

(ii) Identify a change in aggregate demand that might have caused the trend you described above.

Any change that could cause AD to increase, e.g., C ↑, I ↑,
G ↑, or net X↑.

b A downturn in economic activity has an adverse effect on the revenue collected by the government. State an area of government revenue that will be affected and describe why the revenue collected will fall.

Area of revenue affected: direct tax e.g., P.A.Y.E. or corporate tax or GST.

Revenue collected will fall because: P.A.Y.E. – fewer people working or will be working less hours.

Corporate tax – a downturn means small profit for business.

OR – Indirect tax e.g., GST falls because less economic activity means less spending so less GST is collected.

c Place a tick (✓)beside the events that are likely to take place when there is an upturn in economic activity.

(i)	GST receipts for government will increase as household consumption spending increases.	✓
(ii)	Household incomes increase as firms hire extra workers or pay existing workers overtime as they increase production and output.	✓
(iii)	The government operating surplus is likely to increase as tax receipts increase and transfer payments decrease or unemployed individuals get jobs.	✓
(iv)	Government tax receipts fall.	

d (i) List several reasons why government expenses may decrease when there is an upturn in economic activity.

The increase in economic activity and output will provide greater employment opportunities and
therefore less need to pay unemployment benefits.

(ii) Outline why there might not be any decrease in unemployment figures resulting from an increase in economic activity.

Idea that the increase in output and economic activity may be the result of increases in productivity,
greater use of machines/technology or existing workers may be simply doing overtime resulting in
little or no change in employment /unemployment figures.

e How can government spending on Research and Development contribute to growth?

Firms develop new products which increase output/production and growth/new technology linked to
increased production/more efficient production/increases in productivity which increase growth.

> The New Zealand film industry has recently received Government assistance in the form of tax breaks and increased funding.

5 a Explain how Government assistance to the film industry would affect economic growth.

In your answer you should:

- Explain how growth would be affected by increased Government assistance.
- Explain the impact Government assistance for the film industry would have on the wider New Zealand economy.

Government financial assistance and tax breaks will reduce the costs of production for film makers in New Zealand. As costs of production for film makers and the film industry fall firms will increase output, employ more workers and buy capital goods (invest) because they are confident about the future. Overall the impact will see more films produced and growth in the film industry.

Industries that are associated with the film industry in New Zealand will benefit from the flow-on effects of the increase in demand for goods and services required by the film industry. Firms that provide goods or services to the film industry will increase their sales, revenue and profits. These firms will also increase output and aggregate demand will increase. As aggregate demand increases real output GDP will increase, which is economic growth, and there will be an increase in the general price level, which is inflation.

Direct tax cuts …	GST to increase

b Compare and contrast the effects of tax changes on economic activity.

In your answer you should:

- Describe what is meant by a direct tax and explain the effects of direct tax cuts on the economy.
- Describe what is meant by an indirect tax and explain the effect of GST increasing by 1%.

Direct taxes are taxes levied on income or wealth and are paid directly by the taxpayer (individual or company) to the government, for example, income tax and company tax. Direct tax cuts will increase households' disposable income and consumption spending will increase. Firms will increase output to satisfy the increased demand for goods and services. As aggregate demand increases there will be an increase in the general price level (demand-pull inflation) and increase in real GDP (growth).

Indirect taxes are collected by a third party and passed on to the government, for example, GST. An increase in GST will cause an increase in the cost of production. As costs increase, profit will decrease and the aggregate supply curve will shift inward (to the left). This will cause the general price level to increase (cost-push inflation), a decrease in real GDP and, therefore, decreased growth.

    ISBN: 9780170438131

6 Explain the impact of trade on growth.

In your answer you should:

- State the injection flow and withdrawal flow associated with trade.
- Explain how the withdrawal flow would be affected by the upturn in the economy and global boom.
- Explain how the injection flow would be affected by increased global and domestic trade.
- Explain the effect on government operating balance.

The injection flow associated with trade is export receipts while the withdrawal flow is import payments.

An upturn in the global and domestic economies will increase the withdrawal flow because import payments would increase. Many New Zealand firms rely on an imported component in the production process so demand for imported material by New Zealand firms would increase as they produce more to satisfy increased demand for goods and services both locally and from overseas.

An upturn in the global and domestic economies would increase the injection flow because export receipts would increase. Export receipts would increase because New Zealand exporters would be selling/exporting more goods and services to satisfy the increased demand for exports by overseas buyers/consumers.

The government will collect more direct and indirect tax. Direct tax receipts will increase because firms will need to hire extra workers to cope with the increased demand for goods and services. Firms' profits are likely to rise because sales will increase, as will revenue, therefore they will pay more company tax receipts to the government. As households' incomes increase consumption spending will increase and firms will collect more indirect tax receipts (e.g., GST) which they will pass on to the government. As more individuals find jobs, the government will pay less in transfer payments. Overall, the government operating surplus will be a larger surplus or a smaller deficit.

7 a Explain how money spent on education can contribute to growth. Identify the name of the policy that describes increased government spending on education. Explain how increased money spent on education could affect aggregate supply and the inflation rate. Explain how the change in the inflation rate you have described will affect exports, imports and the current account section on the balance of payments.

Increased government spending on education is part of an expansionary fiscal policy.

Increased spending on education will result in a better educated and skilled workforce. A higher skilled workforce will improve productivity which will reduce costs of production for firms. As costs decrease profits increase and the aggregate supply will increase. An increase in aggregate supply will reduce inflationary pressures in the economy.

A fall in the inflation rate in New Zealand will benefit exporters because a decrease in the rate of inflation in New Zealand will mean that New Zealand firms who export will become more price competitive because they are less likely to increase their prices to cover costs and maintain profit margins. Exports will be more price competitive. Export sales are likely to increase causing higher export receipts. Imported products are likely to be less price competitive compared with New Zealand-made products, with consumers buying fewer imports. Overall, as export receipts increase and import payments decrease the current account balance is likely to improve, i.e., be a smaller deficit or greater surplus.

Growth is an objective of government.

b • Explain the impact of increased government spending on growth.
 • Explain why economic growth is an objective of government.

An increase in government spending will inject more money into the economy because money is spent on new projects. Employment will increase and household income increases. Consumption spending will increase. Firms are likely to invest more since business confidence is likely to rise. AD will increase causing the PL to go up and so demand-pull inflation will increase, real output GDP will also increase therefore causing economic growth.

Growth is an objective of government economic policy because it is one of the keys to higher standards of living. Growth has made it possible for people to achieve better living and working conditions, greater life expectancy and a better way of life. For the government it is desirable because it brings in increasing revenues from a given structure of tax rates. It means that more and better roads, schools, hospitals and other social services can be provided without resorting to raising the rates of taxation. Growth can create greater employment opportunities for individuals and unemployment can fall. Economic growth makes it easier for the government to carry out policies of income redistribution and achieve greater equity of income distribution.

     ISBN: 9780170438131

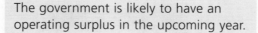
8 Comprehensively explain the effects of a budget surplus on economic activity. In your answer:

- Draw an AD/AS model to depict the New Zealand economy with low levels of unemployment. Label the original equilibrium price PL1 and the equilibrium level of real output Y1.

- Illustrate the effects of an operating balance surplus. Label any curve shifts. Label the new equilibrium price PL2 and new equilibrium level of real output Y2.

- Explain the effect of an operating surplus on the economy, with reference to the graph.

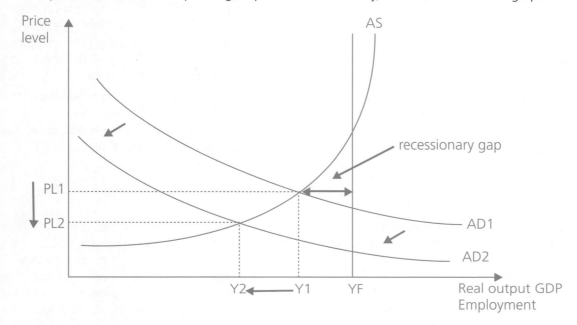

An operating balance surplus will decrease aggregate demand because government withdrawals (taxes/ income) is greater than government injections (government spending/subsidies) so AD shifts inward/left (from AD1 to AD2). Real output GDP/employment will decrease from Y1 to Y2. The price level will decrease from PL1 to PL2.

An operating surplus is likely to see the government increase direct taxes and/or cut transfer payments. Households' disposable incomes will decrease and consumption spending will fall, this will dampen economic activity.

As households spend less, firms' inventories (stock levels) are likely to increase, therefore business confidence may fall and firms invest less because they view the risks of new ventures as higher. A fall in investment spending will further dampen economic activity.

Overall, an operating budget surplus will dampen economic activity resulting in a decrease in inflationary pressures (shown as the decrease in the price level from PL1 to PL2) and decrease employment and real output GDP (as shown as the decrease from Y1 to Y2).

Exchange rates and the TWI

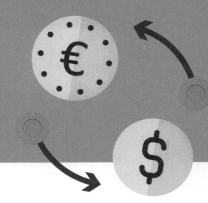

The foreign exchange market

The **foreign exchange market** is the international market in which transactions are conducted to effect the exchange of one national currency for another. When New Zealand exporters earn foreign exchange (forex) these currencies are available to New Zealand importers who need foreign exchange to finance their imports. The market acts as an exchange where foreign and domestic currencies are traded so New Zealand importers can have the yen or pound sterling required to finance their import activities, and New Zealand exporters finish up with the New Zealand dollars they want.

An **exchange rate** is the price at which one currency exchanges for another. An **appreciation** of the exchange rate is when there is a price rise of one currency in terms of another. When $NZ1.00 = $A0.80 ($A = Australian dollar) changes to $NZ1.00 = $A0.84 the New Zealand dollar has appreciated while the Australian dollar has depreciated. A **depreciation** is a fall in the price of one currency in terms of another.

Setting the rate

A **flexible or floating exchange rate** is where the price of currencies, in terms of each other, are determined in the market for foreign exchange. New Zealand has a floating exchange rate that is determined entirely by the demand for and supply of the New Zealand dollar in the foreign exchange market. The demand for and supply of the New Zealand dollar change constantly, so will the value of the New Zealand dollar. The floating of an exchange rate may be a "clean float" when the government does not directly intervene to influence the exchange rate in the foreign exchange market. A "dirty float" is when the the government acts to influence the exchange rate.

Establishing the New Zealand dollar

The New Zealand dollar will depreciate if there is a decrease in demand for it and/or an increase in supply of it in forex markets. A **decrease in demand for the New Zealand dollar** could be due to a decrease in the number of tourists visiting New Zealand. Fewer visitors means there will be less demand for New Zealand dollars in the forex market. A global downturn means that incomes in overseas countries fall, which will result in a decrease in demand for New Zealand-made goods and services therefore less demand for New Zealand dollars in forex markets. Weaker commodity prices will mean that foreign buyers of New Zealand-made goods will need to buy (demand) fewer New Zealand dollars in the forex market to purchase the commodities they require, causing the New Zealand dollar to depreciate.

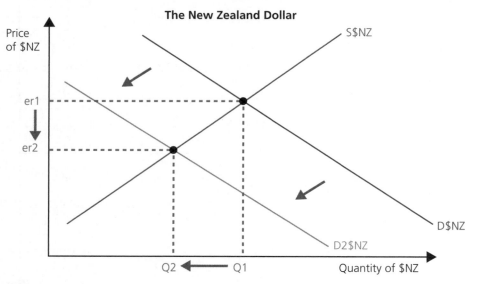

The New Zealand Dollar

The **supply of the New Zealand dollar** will increase when New Zealanders travel overseas because New Zealand travellers will sell (supply) New Zealand dollars to purchase foreign exchange to use in the country or countries they visit. New Zealand firms that import will also need to sell New Zealand dollars to purchase foreign exchange to pay overseas suppliers (firms) in their own currency. Therefore, if New Zealand imports more goods and services, the supply of New Zealand dollars increases in the forex market and the New Zealand dollar will depreciate.

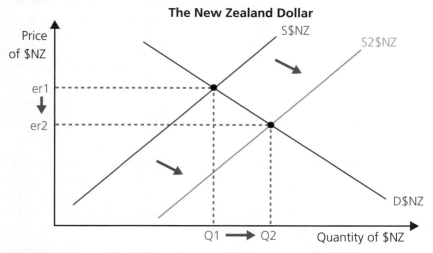

The New Zealand Dollar

Interest rates have a double effect on the exchange rate. When interest rates are high in New Zealand relative to overseas then New Zealand investors will find New Zealand a relatively more attractive place to keep their money. This causes a smaller outflow of the New Zealand dollar and there is a decrease in the supply of it, this causes the New Zealand dollar to appreciate. Overseas investors will be attracted by the returns in New Zealand, and demand for the New Zealand dollar will increase again, causing the dollar to appreciate further.

When interest rates are low in New Zealand relative to overseas then New Zealand investors will find New Zealand a less attractive place to keep their money. This causes an increase in the supply of the New Zealand dollar causing the exchange rate to depreciate. Overseas investors will not be as attracted by the returns on their funds in New Zealand so the demand for the New Zealand dollar will decrease, causing the New Zealand dollar to depreciate further.

Exchange rates – earnings for exporters

To calculate the earnings of an exporter who is paid in a foreign currency, multiply the total currency they receive by (1 divided by the exchange rate). For example, when the exchange rate is NZ$1 equals US$0.80, a New Zealand firm that earns US$200,000 in export income will be paid US$200,000 multiplied by (1/0.8), which equals NZ$250,000. If the exchange depreciates to NZ$1 equals US$0.70, a New Zealand firm earning US$200,000 in export income will now receive US$200,000 multiplied by (1/0.70), which equals NZ$285,714.

Therefore, as the exchange rate depreciates, New Zealand exporters do better because exports are more price competitive and New Zealand exporters would swap foreign exchange for more New Zealand dollars. In this example, a firm that is earning US$200,000 in export income will be NZ$35,714 better off if the exchange rates depreciates from NZ$1 equals US$0.80 to NZ$1 equals US$0.70.

Exchange rates – payment for importers

To calculate the payment that an importer must make in their own currency to pay an overseas firm in its own currency, take the total forex required in payment and divide it by the exchange rate. For example, when the exchange rate is NZ$1 equals US$0.80, a New Zealand firm that imports goods or services from a firm in America worth US$200,000 will need to pay NZ$250,000 (US$200,000 divided by US$0.80). If the exchange depreciates to NZ$1 equals US$0.70, a New Zealand firm that imports goods or services worth US$200,000 will now need to pay NZ$285,714 (US$200,000 divided by US$0.70).Therefore, as the exchange rate depreciates, New Zealand importers will be worse off because imports will cost more. In this example, a New Zealand firm that is paying US$200,000 to an overseas supplier will now need to pay an extra NZ$35,714 when the exchange rates depreciates from NZ$1 equals US$0.80 to NZ$1 equals US$0.70.

Exchange rates and the AD/AS model

Exchange rates have a double impact on the AD/AS model. For example, an appreciation of the New Zealand dollar would make New Zealand exports less price competitive and New Zealand exporters would swap foreign exchange for fewer New Zealand dollars. As incomes (revenue) for exporting firms decrease, this would cause a decrease in aggregate demand (AD) because less income is spent. This will result in a decrease in inflationary pressures. Exporting firms are likely to decrease output because there is less demand from overseas buyers because New Zealand-made products are less price competitive due to the appreciation of the New Zealand dollar. The appreciation would decrease the cost of imported materials, leading to decreased costs of production for firms. As costs fall, profits increase and aggregate supply increases, reducing inflationary pressures. The effect of these changes on real output GDP (economic growth) depends on the relative change between the increase in aggregate supply and the decrease in aggregate demand. Real output GDP may fall, increase or stay the same.

A depreciation of the New Zealand dollar would make New Zealand exports more price competitive and New Zealand exporters would swap foreign exchange for more New Zealand dollars. As incomes (revenue) for exporting firms increase, this would cause an increase in aggregate demand (AD) when this increased income is spent. This will result in an increase in the general price level which is demand-pull inflation. Exporting firms are likely to increase output to satisfy the increase in demand from overseas buyers because New Zealand made products are more price competitive due to the depreciation of the New Zealand dollar. The depreciation would increase the cost of imported materials for New Zealand firms, leading to increased costs of production. As costs increase for firms, profits decrease and the aggregate supply (AS) curve will shift inward (right), so greater cost-push inflation as firms pass on increased costs to consumers by raising prices to maintain profit margins.

Exchange rates, trade and the current account

When the New Zealand dollar appreciates, New Zealand-made goods and services will become more expensive to overseas buyers, New Zealand-made products become less competitive relative to other countries selling the same goods and services, and exports receipts are likely to decrease. Imports will cost less and imports into New Zealand are likely to increase, this could increase import payments. Overall, as export receipts fall and import payments increase it is likely to make the balance on the current account deteriorate, that is a larger deficit or a smaller surplus. However, the impact of an appreciation of an exchange rate on the current account is uncertain because it will depend on the relative change in export receipts and import payments.

A stronger New Zealand dollar will mean it is more expensive for foreign firms or investors to invest in New Zealand therefore decreasing inflows. OR If the New Zealand dollar appreciates then other nations exchange rates depreciate therefore the profit income that arises from New Zealand investments are greater when foreign owned firms or investors swap New Zealand dollars into foreign exchange, so foreign investment in New Zealand inflows increase.

The trade-weighted index (TWI)

The **trade-weighted index (TWI)** measures the value of a currency in terms of a weighted average of the currencies of its major trading partners. The weightings are based on the relative share of each country for New Zealand's overseas trade transactions. They are also weighted against the size of each of these country's GDP.

Time (quarter)	MAR	APR	MAY	Jun	JUL	AUG	SEP
Trade-weighted index monthly							
TWI	55.8	57.8	56.4	60.1	62.1	64.5	66.8

The trade-weighted index should provide a more balanced measure of the strength or weakness of an exchange rate. In the table if the current upward trend for the trade weighted index continues this means the exchange rate is appreciating. This will make exports less price competitive overseas and reduce export receipts. Imports will become cheaper and the country is likely to import more. Less export receipts and more import payments will have a negative impact on the current account balance.

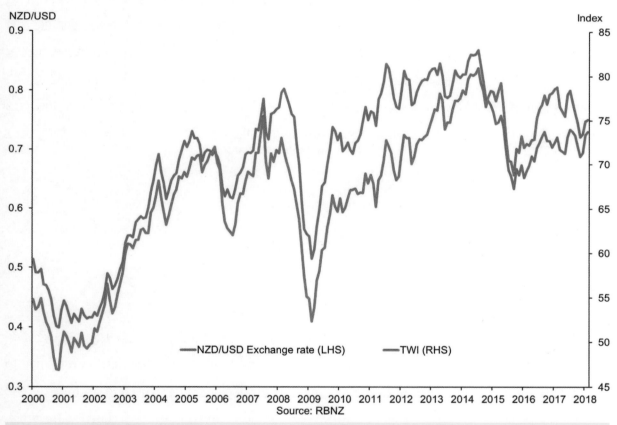

NZ dollar exchange rate & trade-weighted index — monthly average

Source: RBNZ

The nominal TWI series is based on a consistent methodology weighting 17 trading partner currencies using goods and services trade data. The 17 currencies in the TWI basket account for around 85% of New Zealand's foreign trade.

Source: RBNZ

1 a Explain how the value of the New Zealand dollar is established.

The New Zealand dollar is determined by the demand for it and supply of it in the foreign exchange (forex) market.

b Fully explain, with the aid of a diagram, what could cause the value of the New Zealand dollar to appreciate.

The New Zealand dollar will appreciate if there is an increase in demand for it and/or a decrease in supply of it in forex markets. An increase in demand for the New Zealand dollar could be due to an increase in the number of tourists visiting New Zealand. More visitors means there will be greater demand for New Zealand dollars in the forex market. A global upturn means that incomes in overseas countries rise, which will result in an increase in demand for New Zealand-made goods and services therefore greater demand for New Zealand dollars in forex markets. Higher commodity prices will mean that foreign buyers of New Zealand-made goods will need to buy (demand) more New Zealand dollars in the forex market, to purchase the commodities they require, causing the New Zealand dollar to appreciate.

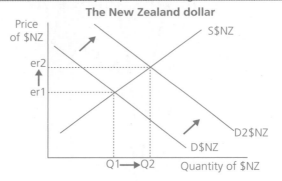

The supply of the New Zealand dollar will decrease when fewer New Zealanders travel overseas because New Zealand travellers will sell (supply) fewer New Zealand dollars to purchase foreign exchange to use in the country or countries they visit. New Zealand firms that import also need to sell New Zealand dollars to purchase foreign exchange to pay overseas suppliers (firms) in their own currency. Therefore, if New Zealand imports fewer goods and services, the supply of New Zealand dollars decreases in the forex market and the New Zealand dollar will appreciate.

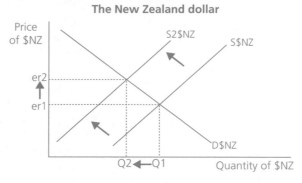

2 **a** On the diagram below, show the impact of an increase in imports on the foreign exchange market. Use appropriate lines, labels and arrows.

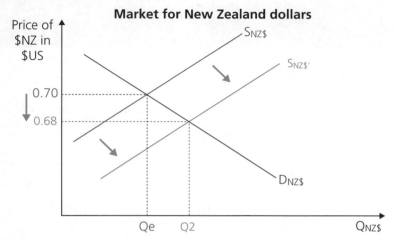

Market for New Zealand dollars

b Complete the table below with a tick (✓) in the appropriate column to indicate if the cause outlined would cause the New Zealand dollar to appreciate or depreciate.

	Cause	Appreciate	Depreciate
(i)	Exports increase	✓	
(ii)	Exports decrease		✓
(iii)	Imports increase		✓
(iv)	Imports decrease	✓	

c Complete the tables

(i)

	Exchange rate	
	NZ$ = AUD $0.90	**NZ$ = AUD $0.80**
Export earnings AUD $100 000	AUD $100 000 x 1/0.90 = NZ$111 111	AUD $100 000 x 1/0.80 = NZ$125 000
Change in export earnings (depreciation)	NZ$13 889 increase	

(ii)

	Exchange rate	
	NZ$ = AUD $0.75	**NZ$ = AUD $0.80**
Import payments AUD $200 000	AUD $200 000 / 0.75 = NZ$266 666	AUD $200 000 / 0.80 = NZ$250 000
Change in import payments (appreciation)	NZ$16 666 decrease	

3 a Complete the table below for the New Zealand dollar in the situations indicated.

Situation	Demand for $NZ and/or supply of $NZ	Direction of shift	Depreciation or appreciation of $NZ
(i) An influx of tourists into New Zealand.	Demand $NZ	Outward	Appreciation
(ii) A decrease in export commodity prices.	Demand $NZ	Inward	Depreciation
(iii) An increase in overseas investors investing in New Zealand-owned businesses.	Demand $NZ	Outward	Appreciation
(iv) Overseas firms repatriate profits back to their own country from New Zealand.	Supply $NZ	Outward	Depreciation
(v) An increase in import commodity prices.	Supply $NZ	Outward	Depreciation
(vi) New Zealand firms set up a factory in South America.	Supply $NZ	Outward	Depreciation
(vii) An increase in interest rates in New Zealand	Demand $NZ	Outward	Appreciation
	Supply $NZ	Inward	Appreciation

b Explain, in detail, how an increase in interest rates would affect the value of the New Zealand dollar.

When interest rates are high in New Zealand relative to overseas then New Zealand investors will find New Zealand a relatively more attractive place to keep their money. This causes a smaller outflow of the New Zealand dollar and there is a decrease in the supply of it, this causes the New Zealand dollar to appreciate. Overseas investors will be attracted by the returns in New Zealand and demand for the New Zealand dollar will increase again, causing the dollar to appreciate further.

c (i) On Graph One, show how an increase in export commodity prices would affect the value of the New Zealand dollar.

Graph One: Market for the New Zealand dollar

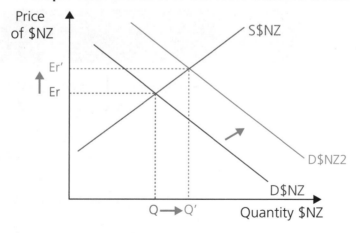

(ii) Explain in detail the change you made in **(i)**.

An increase in export commodity prices will increase demand for $NZ from D$NZ to D$NZ2, causing the New Zealand dollar to appreciate (from Er to Er').

4 **a** Label the axes to illustrate the changes indicated, and then indicate the change on the value of the New Zealand dollar ($NZ).

(i) An increase in revenue received from milk product sales to Korea.

Value of $NZ <u>appreciates</u>

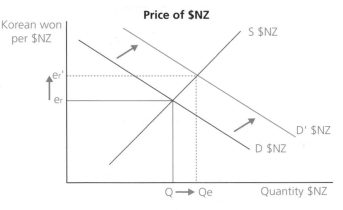

(ii) Upgrading New Zealand army with American-built army personnel carriers.

Value of $NZ <u>depreciates</u>

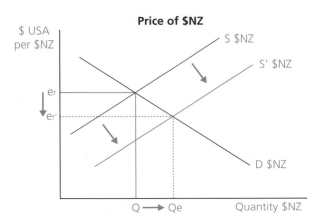

Situation	Demand for $NZ or supply of $NZ?	Direction of shift	Appreciation or depreciation of $NZ?
(i) New Zealand tourists travelling overseas	supply	right	depreciation
(ii) New Zealand importers paying for raw materials	supply	right	depreciation
(iii) New Zealand firm setting up in Fiji	supply	right	depreciation
(iv) The Fijian government buying New Zealand goods and services	demand	right	appreciation
(v) Loss of overseas markets for New Zealand	demand	left	depreciation

c According to the table below, what has happened to the New Zealand dollar in relation to the other currencies?

Currency	Today's rate	Last month's rate
Indonesian rupiah	1 150	1 160
Japanese yen	68	67
US dollar	0.45	0.40
Pound sterling	0.40	0.38

<u>The New Zealand dollar has appreciated against the US dollar, pound sterling and Japanese yen and</u>

<u>depreciated against the Indonesian rupiah.</u>

5 a Describe why it is necessary for New Zealand importers to buy foreign exchange.

So they are able to pay overseas producers for their goods in their own currency; or because overseas producers do not accept New Zealand currency.

b Explain the effect of a fall in the TWI on the current account.

In your answer you should:

- Explain what the TWI measures.
- Explain the effect of a fall in the TWI on New Zealanders travelling overseas and the export sector.
- Explain the impact of a fall in the TWI on the balance of goods.

The Trade-Weighted Index (TWI) measures the New Zealand exchange rate in relation to a basket of currencies (comprising New Zealand's major trading partners/weighted).

A weak New Zealand dollar will mean that New Zealand dollars will be exchanged for less foreign currency. The cost of travelling will rise for New Zealanders and fewer Kiwis will travel because the overseas trip costs more in New Zealand dollars. A weak New Zealand dollar will assist the export sector because overseas buyers find that New Zealand goods and services are cheaper in terms of their currency, or it is cheaper to buy New Zealand dollars to purchase the same amount of New Zealand goods or New Zealand exporters will convert the overseas currency they receive for their goods into more New Zealand dollars than previously received.

If the current downward trend of the TWI continues then this means the New Zealand dollar is depreciating. This will make exports more price competitive overseas and increase export receipts. Imports will become more expensive and New Zealand is likely to import less. Greater export receipts and less import payments will have a positive impact on the balance of goods.

c If the New Zealand dollar depreciated from NZ$1 = AUD$1.00 to NZ$1 = AUD$0.80, calculate the change in earnings for a New Zealand exporter who earns AUD$200 000.

NZ$1 = AUD$1   NZ$1 = AUD$0.80 (OR AUD$200 000 x 1/.80)

NZ$200 000 = AUD$200 000   NZ$1.25 = AUD$1.00

                                              NZ$250 000 = AUD$200 000

Change in earnings: NZ$ 50 000   (Increase) / Decrease   (Circle the correct one)

d Explain the effect a weak New Zealand dollar will have on New Zealanders travelling overseas.

New Zealand dollars will be exchanged for less foreign currency. The cost of travelling will rise for New Zealanders and fewer Kiwis will travel because the overseas trip costs more in New Zealand dollars.

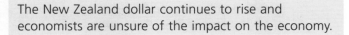

The New Zealand dollar continues to rise and economists are unsure of the impact on the economy.

6 Explain the effect of an appreciation of the New Zealand dollar on the economy.

In your answer you should:

- Use an AD/AS model to illustrate the changes. Label fully.
- Explain the effect of an appreciation on AD and AS.
- Use your graph to explain the overall impact on inflation and growth.

AD/AS model showing the effects on the economy of NZ dollar appreciating

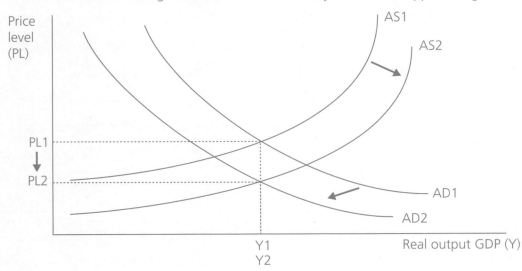

As the New Zealand dollar appreciates exports become less competitive and exporters swap forex for fewer $NZ, so incomes will fall. The AD curve will shift inward.

As the New Zealand dollar appreciates the cost of raw materials are cheaper. This lowers costs of production/ increases profit so the AS shifts to the right as planned output increases.

The AD curve shifting inward has been offset by the AS curve shifting outward, there has been no change in real output GDP (economic growth) because Y1 and Y2 are in the same place on the graph. The general price level has decreased as shown by the change from PL1 to PL2.

Student answers will vary depending on the relative changes to AD and AS.

> A falling dollar is seen as a possible boon for New Zealand exporters

7 a Explain the effect of a falling dollar on exporters.

In your answer you should:

- Explain why a weak dollar is positive for the export industry, including flow-on effects.
- Explain why a weak dollar may not have the expected impact explained above.

A weaker dollar means the New Zealand dollar is depreciating and New Zealand exports will become more price competitive/less expensive to overseas buyers because they would require less foreign exchange to buy the same quantity of exports. Export sales would increase, revenue earned increases and profits could rise. OR exporters would swap forex for more New Zealand dollars in the foreign exchange market so revenues increase. As export incomes increase then firms would be more confident about the future and this would result in an increase in investment spending to make the most of opportunities that are available. Aggregate demand will increase because investment spending and export receipts have increased, therefore there will be an increase in real output GDP (economic growth) and an increase in the general price level (inflation).

The impact explained above might not occur because if there is a worldwide downturn (recession), demand for exports may fall because overseas buyers' incomes have fallen, their consumption spending on imported products may decrease, therefore less New Zealand exports are purchased by overseas buyers. Firms may decide to wait and see instead of investing if they are uncertain about future economic conditions and the higher risks that may be apparent. Fewer exports and less investment will cause AD to shift inward rather than outward, causing reduced inflationary pressure and less growth.

b Complete the tables.

(i)

	Exchange rate	
	NZ$ = US$0.60	**NZ$ = US$0.70**
Export earnings US$250 000	US$250 000 x 1 / .0.60 = NZ$416 666	US$250 000 x 1 / .0.70 = NZ$357 142
Change in export earnings (appreciation)	NZ$59 524 decrease	

(ii)

	Exchange rate	
	NZ$ = US$0.80	**NZ$ = US$0.74**
Import payments US$500 000	US$500 000 / 0.80 = NZ$625 000	US$500 000 / 0.74 = NZ$675 675
Change in import payments (depreciation)	NZ$50 675 increase	

 ISBN: 9780170438131

8 Read the extracts and answer the questions that follow.

> The New Zealand dollar continues to strengthen, now is the time for New Zealanders to travel overseas …

> Profit from exports for firms has fallen because of the high exchange rate as they exchange forex for fewer New Zealand dollars. Firms competing in the domestic market against cheap imports have also experienced falling sales and profit.

a What is meant by the term domestic market?

The New Zealand (onshore) market/the country's market.

b Explain why exporters' profits might be reduced when the exchange rate appreciates.

They receive fewer New Zealand dollars when they exchange the foreign currency they are paid in or

because they become less price competitive with overseas competitors so quantity demanded falls.

c What can New Zealand exporting firms do to stay in business if their profits are reduced by an appreciating exchange rate?

Diversify into other products, find new markets domestically, cut costs, move manufacturing operations

overseas.

d Describe a positive effect of an exporting firm's redundancies for other firms in the economy.

Idea that more labour or resources available.

e (i) Identify several groups who gain from a high exchange rate in New Zealand.

(1) Importers, New Zealanders travelling overseas, consumers

(2) New Zealanders investing abroad.

(ii) Identify several groups who are worse off with a high exchange rate in New Zealand.

(1) Exporters, tourists visiting New Zealand.

(2) Firms that provide goods and services to exporters, New Zealanders who return dividends

from investments abroad.

9 Read the extract and answer the questions that follow.

> The exchange rate was 68.89 United States cents to one New Zealand dollar.
> Today the exchange rate is 70.00 United States cents to one New Zealand dollar.
> Changes in the money market will affect the exchange rate and thereby inflation.

a Given the information above, has the New Zealand dollar strengthened or weakened against the American greenback?

Strengthened

b (i) Sketch and fully label the foreign exchange market for the New Zealand dollar showing an exchange rate of 70 United States cents to one New Zealand dollar.

(ii) Draw on the diagram what will happen to the exchange rate between New Zealand and the United States if New Zealand interest rates rise relative to the United States.

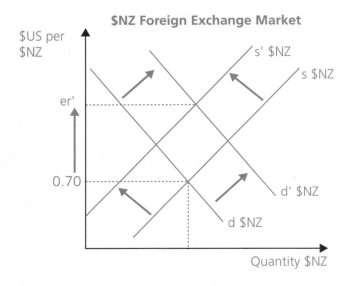

$NZ Foreign Exchange Market

c Explain one effect on inflation that results from a strengthening of the New Zealand dollar.

Prices of imports in $NZ fall, reducing costs (shifting AS outwards) and prices in New Zealand, leading

to a reduction in inflation. The demand for exports will fall leading to a fall in GDP leading to a fall in

demand-pull inflation.

9 MACROECONOMICS
Net exports (X – M) and the current account

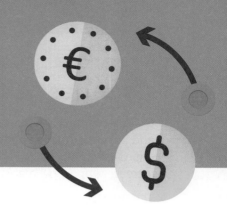

Net exports (X –M)

Net exports (exports minus imports) is a component of aggregate demand. Exports of goods and services (X) represents an inflow (an injection) into a country's circular flow of income and spending adding to aggregate demand. Imports of goods and services (M) represents an outflow (a leakage or withdrawal) from the circular flow of income and spending.

When there is a global downturn or recession, overseas countries' incomes fall resulting in a fall in demand for New Zealand made goods and services. This decrease in exports will affect firms, consumers and the government. As exports decrease New Zealand firms produce fewer goods and services, requiring fewer resources and firms will lay off workers or pay existing workers less overtime. Firms' revenue will fall and they are likely to make smaller profits and pay less company tax. Some firms may close down or look to increase sales in the domestic market. Investment decisions may be put on hold as business confidence falls.

Consumers' incomes will fall because exporting firms will hire fewer workers. The fall in household incomes will result in a fall in consumption spending. Falling business profits will result in less company tax being collected by the government. The decrease in employment results in lower income tax (PAYE) and lower consumer spending will result in less indirect tax being collected. The government will have to pay more in transfer payments.

A decrease in exports will result in a fall in consumption spending and investment. Overall this will decrease aggregate demand causing a decrease in real output GDP (growth) and a fall in the general price level.

The balance of payments

The balance of payments is the account that records all the transactions of one country with the rest of the world. It is divided into three sections. These are the current account, the capital account and the financial account. The **current account** is subdivided into:

- The balance on goods (or merchandise trade balance) – the export of goods minus import of goods, for example, cheese, wool, timber, oil, chemicals, equipment.

- The balance on services – the export of services minus the import of services, for example, transport, insurance, tourism, royalties and government services.

- The balance on income – dividends, interest and profit transmitted between countries. The balance on income for New Zealand has traditionally been a negative figure. This is because foreign-owned firms earn more in New Zealand than New Zealand-owned firms do overseas. New Zealand also has a high degree of foreign debt leading to a large outflow of international investment income.

- The balance of current transfers – includes gifts of goods, services, foreign aid and money sent to relatives and friends overseas.

The current account balance is the sum of the balance on goods, balance on services, balance on income and balance on current transfers. A current account deficit implies New Zealand is spending more money than it is earning from the rest of the world.

Changes in the current account

Changes in the current account are a result of changes in receipts and payments related to imports and exports of goods and services, international investment income, and current transfers. An improvement in the current account (a greater surplus or a smaller deficit) will arise if export receipts increase, import payments fall and/or export receipts rise faster (or fall slower) than import payments.

The quantity of goods and services that New Zealand exports depends on several factors, i.e., the value of the New Zealand dollar, the quality of New Zealand-made products, overseas countries' incomes, tastes and preferences, the price of overseas countries' substitute goods and services. When the New Zealand dollar appreciates, New Zealand goods and services become less price competitive and the quantity demanded for them may fall. As incomes rise in overseas countries then these countries may demand more New Zealand goods and services. The demand for New Zealand dairy and meat products can depend on the perceived real or imagined quality of these products by overseas consumers. Bad press or publicity over the quality of commodities will influence the demand for exports and therefore export earnings.

The quantity of goods imported into New Zealand depends on the factors similar to those that determine the demand for our exports. As New Zealand household incomes rise households may buy a greater number of luxury items such as a new car or electrical goods, or decide to travel.

Economic growth in New Zealand will result in higher disposable incomes with some of this increased income spent on imported goods (e.g., cars, electrical products) and services (e.g., overseas travel), this will impact on the current account.

Inflation in New Zealand will impact on the current account because an increase in the rate of inflation in New Zealand will mean that New Zealand firms will have to increase prices to cover costs and maintain profit margins. As prices increase for New Zealand-made products they will be less price competitive overseas. Export sales are likely to fall causing lower export receipts. Imported products are likely to be more price competitive compared with New Zealand made products, with consumers buying more imports. As import payments increase and export receipts fall the current account balance is likely to deteriorate, i.e., there will be a smaller surplus or greater deficit.

Funding a current account deficit

The current account deficit is funded by borrowing from overseas, this can have a negative effect on economic growth because overseas funds are attracted to New Zealand by higher interest rates in New Zealand relative to those overseas. Higher interest rates in New Zealand are likely to see consumption spending and investment decrease, aggregate demand (AD) shifts inward, resulting in a fall in real output GDP (i.e., growth).

       ISBN: 9780170438131

The capital account

The capital account covers transactions in capital transfers and acquisition disposal of non-produced, non-financial assets. Capital transfers include migrants' transfers, or the assets that people bring with them when they move from one country to another. The outright sale or purchase of an intangible asset such as copyright or a patent is included in the capital account. An example of a non-produced non-financial asset is land, acquisition and disposal is buying and selling.

The financial account

The financial account records transactions involving a country's claims on (assets), and liabilities to, the rest of the world. In the financial account, increases in assets or decreases in liabilities are credit transactions, decreases in assets and increases in liabilities are debit transactions. Financial account transactions are classified according to the type of investment they relate to.

- Direct investment is ownership in another economy that reflects a lasting interest. The definition of direct investment is ownership of 10 percent or more. If a New Zealand company is foreign-owned or if an overseas company is New Zealand-owned then this would be direct investment. Direct investment transactions in the financial account include equity capital, reinvested earnings and other capital. Other capital is the borrowing and lending of funds between the parent and its subsidiary.

- Portfolio investment is separated into equity securities and debt securities. Equity securities denote ownership (less than 10 percent ownership) such as shares. Debt securities are bonds and notes or money market instruments.

- Other investment is a residual investment category. Included in this category are things like loans, trade credits, deposits and any other asset or liability. Trade credits are things like prepayments for goods or services.

- Reserve Assets are special assets held by New Zealand's monetary authority such as foreign currency reserves and Special Drawing Rights (SDRs) with the International Monetary Fund (IMF).

Together the capital account and financial account explain how the current account is financed.

The flow of investment funds

The flow of investment funds in the financial account tends to fluctuate from year to year as foreign investors and New Zealand investors compare the opportunities at home and abroad.

If an economy is buoyant and economic conditions are favourable it is likely a country will attract funds. Investors will view factors such as the security offered, risks involved, the expected rate of return before deciding which international market to invest in and in what form (for example, to buy shares or debt securities such as bonds, notes or other money market instruments).

Investment from investors abroad allows New Zealand to access funds that might otherwise be unavailable in New Zealand. Investment from abroad may provide New Zealand firms with access to the latest technology and expertise that is vital to success or provide an avenue to enter overseas markets (that might otherwise be difficult to access).

Foreign ownership will result in an inflow of capital into New Zealand over a period producing a surplus on the financial account. The ongoing effect of the outflow of profits from New Zealand will produce a decrease in the surplus or an increase in the deficit on the current account.

QUESTIONS & TASKS

1 **a** List the components of the current account balance of the balance of payments.

The balance of goods, the balance of services, the balance on income and the balance on current transfers.

b Which component of the current account would the following transactions be recorded?

	Transaction	Component of current account
(i)	New Zealand apples.	Balance on goods
(ii)	A foreign film crew working in the South Island.	Balance on services
(iii)	Honey from Hawke's Bay.	Balance on goods
(iv)	Competitors for a world championship event in New Zealand.	Balance on services
(v)	Transport by Maesrk (a foreign owned shipping firm).	Balance on services
(vi)	Australian owned bank profits.	Balance on income
(vii)	Dividends earned by overseas shareholders of a New Zealand power company.	Balance on income
(viii)	Dairy products from the Waikato.	Balance on goods
(ix)	Overseas students attending a university in New Zealand.	Balance on services

c State some factors that will determine the level of exports.

The quality of New Zealand made goods and services, overseas countries' tastes and preferences, the price of overseas countries' substitutes, goods and services, the value of the New Zealand dollar, overseas countries' income.

d With reference to low inflation in New Zealand explain how the current account could improve.

Inflation in New Zealand will impact on the current account because a decrease in the rate of inflation in New Zealand will mean that New Zealand firms who export will become more price competitive because they are less likely to increase their prices to cover costs and maintain profit margins. Exports will be more price competitive. Export sales are likely to increase causing higher export receipts. Imported products are likely to be less price competitive compared with New Zealand-made products, with consumers buying fewer imports. Overall, as export receipts increase and import payments decrease the current account balance is likely to improve, i.e., be a smaller deficit or greater surplus.

e Explain the impact New Zealand's distance from world markets has on the current account.

It will contribute to the balance on services with consequently high freight and insurance costs.

       ISBN: 9780170438131

An increase in export receipts will impact on several sectors.

2 a Explain the immediate impact of increased export receipts on the producer sector and explain the flow on effects for consumers, government revenue and the overall level of economic activity in New Zealand.

As exports increase New Zealand firms produce more goods and services, requiring more resources. Firms will hire more workers or pay existing workers more overtime. Firms' revenue will rise and they are likely to make a greater profit and pay more company tax. Some firms will look to invest as business confidence increases.

Consumers' incomes will rise because exporting firms will hire more workers. The increase in household incomes will result in an increase in consumption spending.

Increasing business profits will result in more company tax being collected by the government. Increased employment results in greater income tax (PAYE). Higher consumer spending will result in more indirect tax being collected. The government will pay less in transfer payments.

An increase in exports will result in an increase in consumption spending and investment. Overall this will increase aggregate demand causing an increase in real output GDP (growth) and an increase in the general price level.

b Explain the effects on the current account of a depreciation of the New Zealand dollar compared with an increase in foreign fee-paying students.

In your answer, you should explain in detail:
- how a depreciation of the New Zealand dollar would affect the current account.
- how an increase in foreign fee-paying students would affect the current account.
- why a depreciation of the New Zealand dollar could have a greater impact on the current account than an increase in foreign fee-paying students.

A depreciation of the New Zealand dollar will result in exports becoming more price competitive and exporters will swap forex for more New Zealand dollars. Export receipts are likely to increase. Imports will be expensive, so it is likely that imports will fall then the current account will improve (a greater surplus or smaller deficit).

An increase in foreign fee-paying students will increase export receipts of services (BOS).

A depreciation of the New Zealand dollar is likely to have a greater impact on the current account than an increase in foreign paying students because foreign fee-paying students only affect the balance on services in the current account while a depreciation of the New Zealand dollar will increase export receipts and decrease import payments.

3 a Fully explain how the impact of an increase in government spending on promoting tourism would affect the balance of payments. In your answer you should:

- Explain the effect of increased government spending on tourism promotion on the tourism industry in New Zealand.
- Explain the effects on the current account section of the balance of payments.

When the government increases spending on tourism promotion this will attract overseas visitors to New Zealand as a destination. More firms will set up as tourism operators or existing firms may decide to increase spending on capital goods (investment). An increase in overseas visitors will result in increased sales, revenue and profits for tourist operators as demand for their goods and services increases. There would be greater opportunities for tourist operators because of the increased number of visitors and firms' confidence in the future could result in greater investment, while some firms will hire more workers to cope with increased visitor numbers.

An increase in tourists visiting New Zealand will increase export receipts, therefore the balance on the current account would improve because tourists would improve the balance on services (which is part of the current account).

b Explain the effect of a fall in the TWI on the current account. In your answer you should:

- Explain what the TWI measures.
- Explain the effect of a fall in the TWI on New Zealanders travelling overseas and the export sector.
- Explain the impact of a fall in the TWI on the balance of goods.

The Trade-Weighted Index (TWI) measures the New Zealand exchange rate in relation to a basket of currencies (comprising New Zealand's major trading partners/weighted).

A weak New Zealand dollar will mean that New Zealand dollars will be exchanged for less foreign currency. The cost of travelling will rise for New Zealanders and fewer Kiwis will travel because the overseas trip costs more in New Zealand dollars. A weak New Zealand dollar will assist the export sector because overseas buyers find that New Zealand goods and services are cheaper in terms of their currency, or it is cheaper to buy New Zealand dollars to purchase the same amount of New Zealand goods. New Zealand exporters will convert the overseas currency they receive for their goods into more New Zealand dollars than previously received.

If the current downward trend of the TWI continues then this means the New Zealand dollar is depreciating. This will make exports more price competitive overseas and increase export receipts. Imports will become more expensive and New Zealand is likely to import less. Greater export receipts and lower import payments will have a positive impact on the balance of goods.

Year	Balance on goods $m	Balance on services $m	Balance on income $m	Balance on current transfers $m	Financial account $m	Balance on current account $m
1	1 700	−1 490	−5 000	500	4 825	−4 290
2	500	−680	−5 100	580	5 734	−4 700
3	140	−200	−7 200	370	4 162	−6 890
4	3 680	200	−7 800	370	3 980	−3 550
5	1 800	1 000	−6 700	140	4 786	−3 760

4 a Explain in detail the link between the current account and economic growth.

In your answer you should:

- Fill in the missing values in the table and list the components of the current account. State which column heading in the table is not part of the current account.
- Explain why economic growth might result in a deterioration in the current account.
- Explain why concerns are expressed about the size of New Zealand's current account deficit.

The components of the current account balance are: balance on goods plus balance on services, balance on income and balance on current transfers. The Financial account is not part of the current account.

Economic growth leads to higher disposable incomes leading to higher spending on imports, OR greater demand for materials or equipment from overseas, leading (ceteris paribus) to a deterioration in the current account balance (i.e., a smaller surplus or greater deficit).

The current account deficit is funded by borrowing from overseas, this can have a negative effect on economic growth because overseas funds are attracted to New Zealand by higher interest rates in New Zealand relative to those overseas. Higher interest rates in New Zealand are likely to see consumption spending and investment decrease, AD shifts inward, resulting in a fall in real output GDP (i.e., growth).

Balance of payments New Zealand trade figures $m	Year 1	Year 2	Year 3
Balance on income	−4 900	−6 600	−7 700
New Zealand investment abroad	2 900	5 800	12 000
Foreign investment in New Zealand	5 798	10 000	17 400

b Explain the effect that increasing foreign ownership of New Zealand companies will have on the financial account and on the current account.

Foreign ownership will result in an inflow of capital into New Zealand over a period producing a surplus on the financial account. The ongoing effect of the outflow of profits from New Zealand will produce a decrease in the surplus or an increase in the deficit on the current account.

Balance of payments New Zealand trade figures $m	Year 1	Year 2	Year 3
Balance on income	−4 900	−6 600	−7 700
New Zealand investment abroad	2 900	5 800	12 000
Foreign investment in New Zealand	5 798	10 000	17 400

5 Explain changes in the financial account and its impact on the current account.

In your answer you should:

- Outline several reasons why the flow of investment funds in the financial account tends to fluctuate from year to year.
- Explain why some New Zealand firms have welcomed investment from overseas companies and investors.
- Explain the effect that increasing foreign ownership of New Zealand companies will have on the financial account and on the current account.

Flows of investment funds in the financial account fluctuate from year to year because of the economic climate in New Zealand, availability of funds at home and overseas, changes in interest rates, opportunities for investment in other countries and regulations encouraging or discouraging investment applied by the New Zealand government or overseas governments.

New Zealand firms have welcomed investment from overseas because they are able to access funds or capital goods which they could not otherwise afford, access the latest technology in particular fields, access markets for the output of the enterprise or access managerial expertise (or marketing) which may be lacking, a possible lack of savings in New Zealand means funds aren't available for investment.

Increasing foreign ownership will result in an inflow of capital into New Zealand over a period producing a surplus on the financial account. The ongoing effect of the outflow of profits from New Zealand will produce a decrease in the surplus or an increase in the deficit on the current account.

 ISBN: 9780170438131

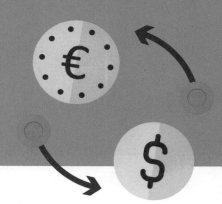

Terms of trade

The **terms of trade** for a country are the ratio of its export prices to its import prices, expressed as an index relative to a base year. The terms of trade can be calculated using the formula below.

Terms of trade = $\dfrac{\text{export price index}}{\text{import price index}}$ x 1000 (or 100)

Changes in our terms of trade depend on relative movements of our export prices to import prices. Price changes in terms of trade can be in the opposite direction, the same direction with one increasing or decreasing faster than the other, or one may be stable and the other changing.

A numerical decrease in our terms of trade is deemed unfavourable while a numerical increase is deemed favourable. The year deemed as most favourable for our terms of trade has the highest index number, while the terms of trade are least favourable in the year with the lowest index number.

When the terms of trade are 1 000, this is the base year for the index from which percentage changes are calculated. The terms of trade index was 1 121 one year relative to a base year, this means that in this year the terms of trade were 12.1% higher than the base year.

An improvement in our terms of trade means a given quantity of our exports will now buy more imports, i.e., the purchasing power of New Zealand exports has increased.

We have to be careful how we view changes in our terms of trade position in relation to our current account balance. A deterioration in our terms of trade because export prices rise slower than the rise in import prices means the purchasing power of our exports has decreased. A given quantity of exports will now buy fewer imports. New Zealand's current account balance could improve if the value of export receipts, are greater than the value of import payments. What is likely to happen if New Zealand's terms of trade index falls is that the import payments will have increased more than export receipts, and the balance of the current account will have worsened (i.e., produced a larger deficit on the current account balance).

There is probably little New Zealand can do to influence its terms of trade, because New Zealand is a small country it must accept the prevailing prices on the world markets.

1 a Define terms of trade.

A ratio of export prices to import prices expressed as an index relative to a base year. The purchasing power of a given quantity of exports.

Terms of trade ended June (1989 = 1 000)	
March years	**Terms of trade**
1992	1 081
1993	1 125
1994	1 118
1995	1 115
1996	1 098

b (i) Referring to the table, a favourable movement in the terms of trade occurred from:

1992 to 1993

(ii) What is the significance of 1989 = 1 000?

This is the base year for the index from which percentage changes are calculated.

c Explain why an improvement in the terms of trade does not necessarily produce an improvement in the balance on the current account.

Recognising that the terms of trade is concerned with the price of exports and imports, while the balance on the current account is concerned with value and volumes, e.g. terms of trade may be improving, but, if export receipts are less than import payments the balance on the current account may deteriorate.

d (i) Calculate the terms of trade in the table below.

Year	Export price index	Import price index	Terms of trade
1987	864	999	865
1988	888	941	944
1989	1 000	1 000	1 000
1990	1 064	1 034	1 029
1991	1 084	1 040	1 042

(ii) What is the base year? 1989

(iii) In which year were the terms of trade the:

most favourable? 1991   least favourable? 1987

(iv) What does an index number of 1 042 mean relative to the base year?

In that year the terms of trade were 4.2% higher than the base year.

2 Refer to the information in the table and answer the questions that follow.

	Quarter	
	Year 1 June	**Year 1 September**
Export Receipts ($m, year to date)	29 800	30 000
Import Payments ($m, year to date)	33 000	34 000
Exports Volume Index	1 040	950
Imports Volume Index	1 400	1 370
Terms of Trade	1 090	1 080
Current Account Balance (% of GDP, year to date)	–5.0	–6.0
Exchange Rate (TWI)	65.1	68.2

a What does the information on export receipts and export volumes indicate has happened to export prices in the September quarter?

The increase in export receipts while export volumes decreased indicates that export prices have

increased.

b Refer to the change in the terms of trade to describe what must have happened to import prices in the September quarter.

The fall in the terms of trade indicates that import prices have increased at a faster rate than export

prices.

c Use the information on import payments and volumes to justify your answer to **b**.

The increase in import payments while import payments volumes decreased indicates that import prices

have increased. OR, the use of data to show that the rise in import prices is proportionately more than

export prices.

d In the quarter to December Year 1 the TWI increased to 71.5. Explain what you would have expected to happen to export receipts, import payments, and the current account deficit.

E.g., Export receipts would fall, because items sold in foreign currencies return fewer NZ$ to exporters

when the $NZ appreciates. Import payments would rise because cheaper imports will result in extra

spending. The current account deficit would worsen/increase.

3 a Indicate if the following statements are correct or incorrect.

	Statement	Correct or incorrect
(i)	Export and import prices can change simultaneously and not necessarily in the same direction.	correct
(ii)	New Zealand relies on its export income to purchase imports and for any given quantity of export, total income must be affected by prices.	correct
(iii)	If New Zealand's terms of trade become unfavourable, a given quantity of exports will buy less imports than it used to.	correct
(iv)	The terms of trade reflect the quantities of goods and services traded.	incorrect
(v)	If New Zealand's volume of trade is relatively stable then an improvement (or favourable movement) in the terms of trade is likely to result in a positive movement in the balance of goods.	correct
(vi)	New Zealand as a small country usually has little or no control over prices when selling and buying on international markets.	correct

Assume that New Zealand's terms of trade have improved.

b Read the extract and answer the questions that follow.

(i) Explain what is meant by the idea that 'New Zealand's terms of trade have improved'.

An improvement in the terms of trade means that the purchasing power of our exports has improved, i.e., it takes fewer exports to pay for the given unit of imports.

(ii) Explain one positive impact and one negative impact of an improvement in New Zealand's terms of trade.

Positive impact: The Balance on Goods is likely to improve (assuming stable volumes of exports and imports) as export receipts increase at a greater rate than import payments. Businesses are likely to expand and employ more workers. Government tax revenue will rise from company taxes, increased PAYE because of higher employment levels.

Negative impact: Economic growth is likely to increase resulting in inflationary pressures in the economy. Interest rates may rise with inflationary pressures. This will increase the cost of borrowing, credit cards.

(iii) Draw a conclusion as to whether or not an improvement in New Zealand's terms of trade is beneficial for the economy.

New Zealand is likely to be better off with business expansion, economic growth and job opportunities, there may be some pressures on prices (inflation).

 ISBN: 9780170438131

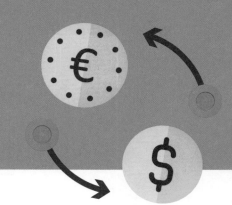

Income/consumption and savings

Individuals' income (Y) can either be consumed (C) or saved (S). We are concerned with marginal analysis and the following ideas are used. **Marginal propensity to consume** (**MPC**) is the proportion of the last unit of income spent on consumption. If 80 cents of the last dollar of income is used for consumption expenditure, then MPC = 0.8. **Marginal propensity to save** (**MPS**) is the proportion of the last unit of income that is saved. If 20 cents of the last dollar is used in this way, then MPS = 0.2. MPC plus MPS always equals 1. The diagram below shows the change that occurs when private final expenditure increases by $100m due to, say, tax cuts. In practice individuals save some of the income and spend the rest. The portion that is spent becomes income for someone else. They also save a portion of this and spend the rest. In this way the process repeats itself and incomes spread throughout the economy. The expansion process is governed by both the portion spent and the part withdrawn (or saved). In our example the only leakage from the spending stream is saving.

Because of the subsequent rounds of spending, GDP increases by more than the original amount spent; this is a multiplied amount, as shown in the example below.

The multiplier process

Income (Y)	=	Consumption (C)	+	Savings (S)		
$100m	=	$80m	+	$20m		
Y	=	C	+	S		
$80m	=	$64m	+	$16m		
Y	=	C	+	S		
$64m	=	$51.2m	+	$12.8m		
Y	=	C	+	S	
$51.2m	=	$40.96m	+	$10.24m	

The initial spending increases economic activity (GDP or incomes) by the full $100m. The secondary round of spending led to an increase of $80m and subsequent rounds of $64m and $51.2m. This process continues until changes in incomes (Y) become so small that they can be ignored. In our example GDP will eventually increase by $500m. Any given increase (or decrease) in spending will cause a more than proportionate change in GDP, that is, a multiplied effect. We use the term 'multiplier' to imply that a change in GDP will be a multiplied change of the change that caused it.

We can calculate the size of the basic multiplier from the formula given below and size of the change in income (or GDP).

The **size of the basic multiplier** = 1 / 1-c = 1 / 1-0.8 = 1 / 0.2 = 5 times, where c = MPC

We can further calculate the multiplied effect on the level of income using the formula below.

The change in income (or GDP) = change in spending × multiplier

= $100m × 5

= $500 million

A worked example

If the MPC equals 0.75 and household spending decreases by $50 million, the decrease in GDP can be calculated as follows.

The size of the multiplier = 1 / 1 - c = 1 / 1 - 0.75 = 1 / 0.25 = 4 times, where c = MPC

The change in income (or GDP) = change in spending × multiplier

= $50 million × 4

= $200 million decrease in GDP

Eliminating a deflationary gap

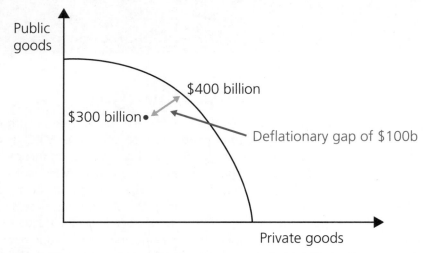

The diagram shows an economy whose maximum output is $400 billion. The economy is currently operating at $300 billion. To eliminate the deflationary gap of $100 billion it does not require that spending increases by the full $100 billion because of the multiplier idea. If the MPC was 0.8 then the multiplier would be 5 times. In order to close the gap of $100 billion spending need only have to increase initially by $20 billion, as the subsequent round of spending will see GDP (or incomes) increase by $100 billion.

A worked example

To eliminate a deflationary gap of $320 million when the MPC is 0.75, government spending would need to increase by only $80 million. This is shown in the working below.

The formula to use:

The size of the deflationary gap = The change in spending x the multiplier

Substitute the values given in the questions.

$320m = $80m x the multiplier (1/1 − c)

$320m = $80m x 4 (because 1/1 − c = 1/1 − 0.75 = 4x)

QUESTIONS & TASKS

1 a (i) Complete the table and the statement that follows.

MPC	Working		Size of the multiplier
0.9	$\dfrac{1}{1-.9}$	$= \dfrac{1}{.1}$	10 x
0.8	$\dfrac{1}{1-.8}$	$= \dfrac{1}{.2}$	5 x
0.75	$\dfrac{1}{1-.75}$	$= \dfrac{1}{.25}$	4 x
0.6	$\dfrac{1}{1-.6}$	$= \dfrac{1}{.4}$	2.5 x

(ii) The multiplier will be larger, the <u>larger (bigger) the MPC</u>

b (i) Complete the table.

Information	Size of the multiplier			Size of the change in GDP
Government increases spending in healthcare by $150m when MPC = 0.75	$\dfrac{1}{1-.75}$	$= \dfrac{1}{.25}$	$= 4$ x	4 x $150m = $600M
Investment by firms increases by $80m when MPC = 0.9	$\dfrac{1}{1-.9}$	$= \dfrac{1}{.1}$	$= 10$ x	10 x $80m = $800M

(ii) The multiplier is smaller if l<u>   leakages   </u> of taxation or i<u>   imports   </u> are included.

(above "leakages": withdrawals)

c Tick (✓) which of the following are leakages from the spending stream in the multiplier process.

Taxes	✓	Investment by firms	
Household sepnding		Exports	
Savings	✓	Imports	✓

2 a Complete the statement below on the multiplier effect.

People can either spend (c_____consume_____) or s_____save_____ their income. We can write:

Y	=	C	+	S
Income	=	Consumption	+	Savings

Any chnge in income will result in changes in both c_____consumption_____ and s____savings____,

i.e. $\Delta Y = \Delta C + \Delta S$. If we divide both sides by change in Y we get

$1 = \dfrac{\Delta C}{\Delta Y} + \dfrac{\Delta S}{\Delta Y}$. We call $\dfrac{\Delta C}{\Delta Y}$ the marginal propensity to consume (MPC)

while $\dfrac{\Delta S}{\Delta Y}$ is called the marginal propensity to save (MPS)_____.

From our workings we can deduce that a change in income results in a change in the tendency to consume and save with a proportion on each; we can deduce that MPC plus MPS equals _____1_____.

If consumers receive an extra $200m due to cuts in direct tax some of this is spent and the rest is

s____saved____. The spending of one person is someone else's i____income____, which is then spent

and saved. If MPC = 0.80 and MPS = _____0.20_____, the effects of the $200m on incomes is shown

below.

Income (Y)	=	Consumption (C)		+	Savings (S)
$200m	=	$160m		+	_____$40M_____
		_____$160m_____ =	_____$128m_____	+	_____$32M_____
			_____$128m_____ =	_____$102.4M_____ +	_____$25.6M_____

The original spending has had a m_____multiplied_____ effect (more than p____proportionate____)

increase in GDP. We can work out the size of the change in GDP by using the formula below.

$\Delta \text{ income} = \Delta \text{ spending} \times \dfrac{1}{1 - MPC} \ \left(\text{or } \dfrac{1}{MPS}\right)$

This is the simple multiplier (basic) as it only considers the leakage from the spending process of

s _savings_____.

The full multiplier considers leakages or w_____withdrawals_____ from the spending stream of

t_taxes_____ and i____imports____ payments. Allowing these leakages would r_reduce_____ the

size of the multiplier.

b Complete the table.

	Change in spending	MPC	Multiplier	Change in GDP
(i)	Government spending increases by $4 billion.	0.80	5x	$20 billion increase
(ii)	Investment spending decreases by $2 billion.	0.75	4x	$8 billion increase
(iii)	Consumption spending increases by $150 million.	0.80	5x	$750m increase

3 a Complete the table.

Change in spending	MPC	Multiplier	Change in GDP
(i) Investment spending increases by $1 billion.	0.90	10x	$10 billion increase
(ii) Government spending decreases by $5 billion.	0.50	2x	$10 billion decrease
(iii) An additional $50 billion of spending.	0.70	3.33	$166.67 billion increase

b (i) There is an increase in additional spending of $4.5 billion after a major earthquake that destroys roads and infrastructure. Calculate the change in real GDP that would occur if the MPC was 0.95.

(ii) Show the impact on the AD/AS model below of the increase in additional spending. Label the changes fully.

(iii) Explain the impact of the additional spending on economic growth and full employment in the economy.

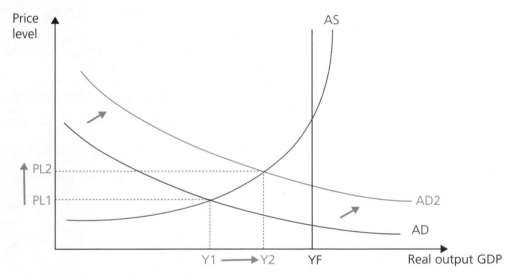

The multiplier equals 1/ 1 − 0.95 = 20 x. Real output GDP would increase by $90 billion ($4.5b x 20) from the additional $4.5 billion spending because this increased spending by households and firms would be income for others, which then is spent becoming income for others.

The building of new roads, bridges and infrastructure requires that firms employ extra workers. This would increase the incomes of households which then would be spent, insurance pay outs to fix homes/driveways/garages would also be spent.

Investment spending by firms would increase because firms would need to buy more capital goods to carry out the construction required or to replace old equipment. Therefore, consumption spending and investment spending increases, AD would increase with the aggregate demand curve shifting outward as shown as the shift from AD to AD2. Real output GDP would increase, as shown as the increase from Y to Y2, this indicates economic growth. Employment would increase because as output increases firms need additional workers.

4 a The spending multiplier equals 1/1 minus the MPC. Use the spending multiplier to explain how an increase in investment spending of $8 billion can result in an increase in Gross Domestic Product of $32 billion.

A given increase in spending will cause a more than proportionate increase in GDP, that is, a multiplied effect. The multiplier must be 4 so 1/(1 – MPC) equals 4. 1 – MPC equals 0.25, MPC equals 0.75 or MPS equals 0.25. The initial spending (injection) increases economic activity (GDP or incomes) by the full $8b. This $8b becomes the income of firms and households. Of this $8b there is a secondary round of spending of $6b, and subsequent rounds of $4.5b and $3.375b. This process continues until the change in incomes (Y) becomes so small that it can be ignored. In this instance GDP will eventually increase by $32b.

b Given the spending multiplier is initially 4, explain the impact on the size of the multiplier and economic activity of an increase in interest rates.

(i) With reference to consumption and savings, explain in detail how an increase in interest rates can have multiplied effects on the economy.

A household can either spend or save the income it receives. Consumption spending (C) is household spending on goods and services and is likely to decrease when interest rates increase because there is a greater incentive to save. If interest rates increase then it is likely that fewer households take out loans to buy items they desire, do renovations to houses or buy a property (home), this will decrease consumption spending. The sacrificing of present consumption is savings (S) because it represents income not spent.

(ii) With reference to the multiplier explain how an increase in interest rates would impact on economic growth, inflation and employment.

As interest rates increase, individuals are more likely to save because they are receiving a higher return on funds put aside to use later. Higher interest rates decrease consumption spending by households, this will decrease the income of firms because the portion of income that is spent becomes income for someone else. If there is a decrease in incomes then this will result in a decrease in income for someone else. In this way the process repeats itself and there will be a decrease in incomes spread throughout the economy. The contraction process is governed by both the portion spent and the part withdrawn (or saved). As savings increase the marginal propensity to save (MPS) will increase. When the MPS increases the spending multiplier will decrease, this will decrease the multiplier effect to below 4. Economic growth will decrease as output falls and there will be fewer inflationary pressures in an economy. Employment will fall and unemployment will increase because as output falls firms will require fewer workers.

5 **a** The spending multiplier equals 1/1 minus the MPC. Use the spending multiplier to explain how an increase in government spending of $10 billion can result in an increase in Gross Domestic Product of $50 billion.

A given increase in spending will cause a more than proportionate increase in GDP, that is, a multiplied effect. The multiplier must be 5 so 1/ (1 – MPC) equals 5. 1 – MPC equals 0.2, MPC equals 0.8 or MPS equals 0.2. The initial spending (injection) increases economic activity (GDP or incomes) by the full $10b. This $10b becomes the income of firms and households. Of this $10b there is a secondary round of spending of $8b, and subsequent rounds of $6.4b and $5.12b. This process continues until the change in incomes (Y) becomes so small that they it can be ignored. In this instance GDP will eventually increase by $50b.

b When the MPC for a country is 0.90, a tax refund of $150m to households will eventually lead to and actual increase in GDP of: **(i)** $150m **(ii)** something less than $1 500m **(iii)** something more than $1 500m **(iv)** exactly $1 500m

(ii) something less than $1 500m. The change in GDP can be calculated using this formula, the size of the multiplier multiplied by the change in spending, 10 multiplied by $150m equals $1 500m. However this calculation is based on the assumption that there are no further leakages apart from savings. Further leakages will mean the change in GDP will not be as much.

c If there is additional spending of $80 million per year and households spend 95% of their income, calculate the multiplied effect that this spending has on the economy.

The multiplied effect that this spending has on the economy equals 1/ (1 minus the MPC) multiplied by the change in spending. 1/ (1 – 0.95) multiplied by $80m equals $1 600m.

d There will be a multiplier of 4 if the marginal propensity to consume is:

75%. The size of the multiplier = 1 / 1 – c = 1 / 1 – 0.75 = 1 / 0.25 = 4 times, where c = MPC

e Explain why there is a small but significant difference between the multiplier effect of an increase in government spending of $100m and that of a similar decrease of $100m in direct taxes.

This is because part of the $100m reduction in taxes does not increase spending by the full $100m because some proportion is saved. The $100m increase in government spending has a greater multiplier effect than if taxes were to be decreased by the same amount.

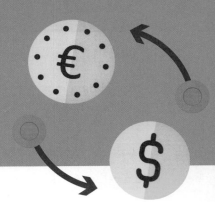

12 MACROECONOMICS
Monetary policy

Monetary policy

Monetary policies are policies used by the government to control the price (and quantity) of money and credit available to the economy to achieve its economic goals. In New Zealand The Governor of the Reserve Bank is charged with keeping inflation between 1% and 3% (on average over the medium term) as outlined in its Policy Target Agreement (PTA). This is also linked to sustainable economic growth, employment and development.

A tool that a Central Bank can use to carry out monetary policy is the Central Bank interest rate. In New Zealand this is termed the **Official Cash Rate (OCR)**. The OCR is the overnight interest rate target that a Central Bank can use to control the price of money. The OCR is the interest rate set by a country's Central Bank for registered banks on their settlement cash deposits. In New Zealand the Reserve Bank will pay interest at 0.25% lower than the OCR to registered banks for their settlement cash deposits and is prepared to lend to registered banks at 0.25% above the OCR if registered banks need to borrow from the Reserve Bank of New Zealand to fund their settlement cash deposits. In this way the OCR will influence the call rate and interest rates. Market interest rates are generally held around the Central Banks key interest rate.

AD/AS: Loose (expansionary) monetary policy

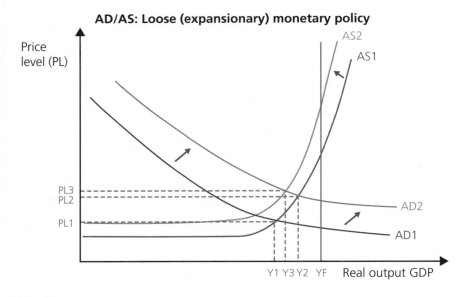

Loose monetary policy is used when the level of economic activity is below potential, and there are signs that the level of prices may fall with the possibility of deflation taking place. Loose (expansionary) monetary policy involves a Central Bank decreasing base rates. This will cause banks to decrease their retail interest rates.

As interest rates decrease, consumption spending should increase because the cost of credit has decreased, and households will have less incentive to save because they are receiving a lower return, both of these are likely to increase aggregate demand (AD). Investment spending by firms will increase because the cost of borrowing is lower meaning the risks of new ventures will be lower and the returns more profitable, this will cause AD and output to increase. Overall, loose (expansionary) monetary policy will stimulate economic activity resulting in an increase in inflationary pressures (shown as the increase in the price level from PL1 to PL2) and increase employment and real output GDP (as shown as the increase from Y1 to Y2).

As interest rates decrease an exchange rate for a country is likely to depreciate because the demand for its currency will decrease because overseas investors will be less attracted by the lower returns on their funds.

       ISBN: 9780170438131

The supply of the currency will increase on the foreign exchange market because investors from that country will look to invest their funds off-shore rather than invest domestically. As the exchange rate depreciates exports will become more price competitive and exporters will swap foreign exchange for more of their own currency. As exporters' incomes increase, aggregate demand will increase. As the currency depreciates imports will cost more. As firms' costs of production increase, profits will decrease, this will cause the aggregate supply curve will shift inward (from AS1 to AS2) which will increase the price level (PL2 to PL3) and decrease real output GDP (Y2 to Y3).

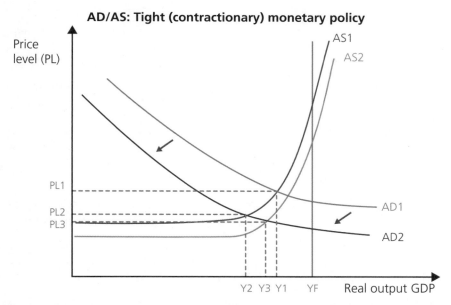

AD/AS: Tight (contractionary) monetary policy

When the economy is operating close to full employment and there are inflationary pressures, tight monetary policy is used to dampen economic activity. A restrictive **monetary policy (tight or contractionary)** involves an increase in the base rate by a Central Bank. Banks will raise their retail interest rates causing consumption spending to fall because the cost of credit has increased, households will have a greater incentive to save because they are receiving a higher return. Investment spending by firms will decrease because the cost of borrowing is higher meaning the risks of new ventures are higher and the returns less profitable. Both these events cause a decrease in aggregate demand and output. Overall, tight (contractionary) monetary policy will dampen economic activity resulting in a decrease in inflationary pressures (shown as the decrease in the price level from PL1 to PL2) and decrease employment and real output GDP (as shown as the decrease from Y1 to Y2).

As interest rates increase an exchange rate for a country is likely to appreciate because the demand for its currency will increase because overseas investors will be attracted by the relatively higher returns on their funds. The supply of the currency will decrease on the foreign exchange market because investors from that country will look to invest their funds on-shore rather than off-shore. As the exchange rate appreciates exports will become less price competitive and exporters will swap foreign exchange for less of their own currency. As exporters' incomes decrease, aggregate demand will decrease. As the currency depreciates imports will cost less. As firms' costs of production decrease, profits will increase, this will cause the aggregate supply curve will shift outward (from AS1 to AS2) which will decrease the price level further from PL2 to PL3, and increase real output GDP from Y2 to Y3.

A Central Bank could also reduce inflationary pressures in an economy by selling government securities via its Open Market Operations (OMO) or by issuing statements (moral suasion) on monetary conditions. This may head interest rates in the direction that the Central Bank requires.

Changes in interest rates will impact on the level of savings, consumption spending, investment and the exchange rate and therefore on the level of inflation, growth and employment in an economy. However, the changes in consumer and producer responses to an increase or decrease in the OCR may not be as expected or predicted because there may be a 'time lag', a delay of time between the announcement of a change to the OCR and the interest rates that apply to households and firms. Sometimes it takes time for banks to pass on cuts in interest rates to their customers. Also, when interest rates change there are households and firms that have fixed term mortgages so the change in the interest rates has no effect on them. If households are concerned about the future and want to reduce debt then lower interest rates may not have such a stimulatory effect if households decide to save more and spend less. Firms may invest more despite an increase in interest rates because they are confident about the future and view the venture they are undertaking as being profitable.

1 a (i) Which institution is given responsibility for keeping prices stable in New Zealand?

The Reserve Bank of New Zealand.

(ii) Identify the agreement between the Minister of Finance and the institution in (i) that specifies the inflation target.

Policy Target Agreement.

(iii) What is the current inflation target specified in the agreement?

1% to 3% over the medium term on average.

b (i) What is the name given to the system currently in place for the Reserve Bank of New Zealand's operation of monetary policy? How does it work when inflationary pressures are evident?

Policy: Official Cash Rate, which is the overnight interest rate on money the RBNZ lends to, or borrows from commercial banks. It is reviewed regularly (every six weeks) and adjusted if the RBNZ considers there are inflationary or deflationary pressures in the economy.

Inflationary pressures: The RBNZ increases the OCR, and hence the interest rate structure in the economy, investment and consumption will be discouraged therefore easing inflationary pressures. Export demand is likely to fall because increased interest rates will cause the New Zealand dollar to appreciate.

(ii) State one other policy tool the Reserve Bank of New Zealand could use to control inflation.

Open market operations, moral suasion, jawboning.

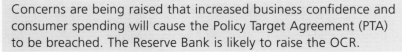

> Concerns are being raised that increased business confidence and consumer spending will cause the Policy Target Agreement (PTA) to be breached. The Reserve Bank is likely to raise the OCR.

2 Explain why the Policy Target Agreement might be breached and the likely government response.

In your answer you should:

- State the target range for the PTA and explain why it could be breached.
- Explain the government policy that could be used to achieve the target set and its effect on interest rates, consumption spending, investment and net exports.

The target range for the PTA is to keep (CPI) inflation between 1% and 3% (per annum) on average over the medium term. The concern for the Reserve Bank is that increased consumer and investment spending will cause aggregate demand to increase and cause the general price level (inflation) to rise beyond the target range set.

The government policy to deal with breaches of the PTA is tight (contractionary) monetary policy and will result in an increase in the Official Cash Rate (OCR). As the OCR increases so will banks' retail interest rates. Consumption spending will decrease as interest rates increase because there is a greater incentive to save. The increased cost of borrowing will result in consumers borrowing less and a decreased use of credit spending. Those households with a variable mortgage will pay more in interest, reducing funds available for spending. Aggregate demand (AD) will therefore decrease, reducing inflationary pressures.

Investment spending by firms will decrease because the higher cost of borrowing will increase the risks and reduce the profitability of new ventures. As less capital is purchased, aggregate demand will fall, reducing inflationary pressures. Higher interest rates will cause the NZ$ to appreciate. Exports will become less price competitive and exporters will swap forex for fewer NZ dollars, so export receipts will fall. Therefore aggregate demand falls, reducing inflationary pressures.

3 a What is meant by an Official Cash Rate of 5.25%?

It is the price of money set by the RBNZ which is prepared to supply unlimited quantities of money to the banking system at 0.25% above the OCR.

b Give one reason the Official Cash Rate may not be altered further, despite the fact that inflation is outside the target range.

Valid reason related to ideas like PTA requires inflation to be between 1–3% on average in the medium term. Time lags mean the effect of past increases or decreases have not fully impacted on the rate of inflation.

> A decrease in interest rates will have a significant impact on consumers and producers, and therefore on economic activity.

c Compare and contrast the impact of a decrease in interest rates on economic activity.
In your answer you should:
- Explain the effect of a decrease in interest rates on consumers and producers.
- Explain why the changes may not be as significant as you predict.

As the OCR decreases interest rates would fall. Household consumption spending would increase because savings would decrease as households receive lower returns. Borrowing would increase because the cost of a loan would fall. As some households pay less on mortgage repayments, their discretionary incomes would increase and increase the funds they have to spend or save. These changes will cause AD to shift outward.

As interest rates fall firms are likely to increase spending on capital goods because the lower cost of borrowing will reduce the risks involved and increase the profitability of new activites. AD will shift outward. The decrease in interest rates is likely to cause the dollar to depreciate. Firms that export will find that their products are more price competitive and they are able to swap forex for more $NZ. Incomes of exporters increase, causing AD to shift outward.

The changes in consumer and producer responses to a decrease in the OCR may not be as significant as I predicted because there will be a 'time lag', i.e., there will be a delay of time between the announcement of a change to the OCR and the effect on interest rates that apply to households and firms. Also, when interest rates fall, some households and firms have fixed mortgages so the change in the OCR has no effect on them. Firms will not necessarily invest more as interest rates fall because they may not be confident about the future and unwilling to take the risk of investing despite the cheaper loans available.

4 a (i) Use the data in the table to discuss how effective monetary policy has been in achieving its primary objective.

Year	C P I % change	Policy target agreement
1	0.4	0–3%
2	0.5	0–3%
3	–0.7	0–3%
4	1.8	0–3%
5	2.7	1–3%
6	2.5	1–3%
7	4.1	1–3%

The percentage change in the CPI inflation rate has been within the limits set by the PTA for all but

two years (Years 3 and 7) so monetary policy has been successful in achieving its main objectives.

(ii) Explain what happened in Year 3.

The general (average) price level fell by 0.7% – i.e., there was deflation, inflation was a negative.

b (i) Why might an increase in the OCR cause the exchange rate to appreciate?

Higher interest rates in New Zealand will attract overseas savers/investors to New Zealand

increasing demand for NZ$. This decreases supply of NZ$ in the Foreign Exchange Market causing

the exchange rate to rise/appreciate.

(ii) How does an increase in the OCR impact on the inflation rate in New Zealand. Relate your answer to a change in the value of the New Zealand dollar?

The Reserve Bank will increase the OCR/increase interest rates, exchange rates will appreciate/

exporters' incomes will fall so less demand-pull inflation/imports cheaper so less cost-push inflation.

Less upward pressure on prices/less inflationary pressure/lower prices.

5 Explain the effect of a cut in the interest rates on inflation and economic growth.
In your answer you should:

- Draw and fully label an AD/AS model to show the effects of interest rate cuts.
- Explain the effect on households and firms.
- Explain the overall effect on inflation and economic growth.

Effect of interest rate cuts on the AD/AS model

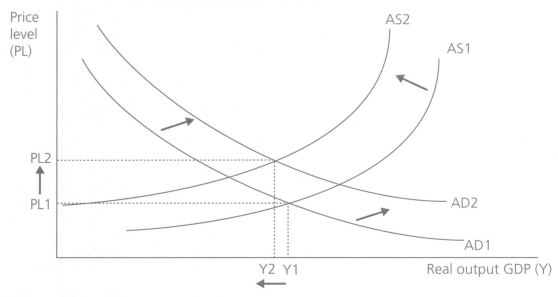

When interest rates decrease household consumption spending would increase because savings would decrease as households receive lower returns. Borrowing would increase because the cost of a loan would fall. Since some households pay less on mortgage repayments, their discretionary incomes would increase and increase the funds they have to spend or save. These changes will cause AD to shift outward from AD1 to AD2. As interest rates fall firms are likely to increase spending on capital goods because the lower cost of borrowing will reduce the risks involved and increase the profitability of new activities. AD will shift outward.

The decrease in interest rates is likely to cause the dollar to depreciate. Firms that export will find that their products are more price competitive and they are able to swap forex for more $NZ. Incomes of exporters increase, causing AD to shift outward. As the exchange rate depreciates the cost of imported raw materials increases. This increases costs of production/decreases profit so the AS curve shifts inward as planned output decreases.

The overall impact is an increase in the general price level as shown in the increase from PL1 to PL2. On the diagram there is a fall in real output GDP, shown as the decrease from Y1 to Y2, therefore a fall in economic growth.

6 Comprehensively explain how the Reserve Bank of New Zealand targets inflation using the Official Cash Rate. In your answer you should:

- Explain how the OCR is used to achieve price stability.
- Explain how the change in the OCR will affect the balance of trade and employment.
- Justify the government keeping prices stable from a trade perspective.

Price stability as currently defined in the Policy Target Agreement is to keep inflation between 1% and 3% (on average over the medium term). RBNZ increases the OCR, increasing interest rates, the exchange rate will appreciate, exporters' incomes will fall so less demand-pull inflation, imports will be cheaper so less cost-push inflation, less upward pressure on prices. As the RBNZ increases the OCR, increasing interest rates, people will borrow less, save more, pay more interest on existing loans, firms will borrow less, invest less, decrease in consumer spending, less demand for goods and services, less upward pressure on prices.

As the OCR increases, interest rates increase. High interest rates cause the exchange rate to appreciate. Exports will be less (price) competitive/more expensive, while imports will be more (price) competitive/cheaper. Export receipts fall and import payments rise. Therefore, the Balance of Trade will get worse, i.e., a smaller surplus or greater deficit. Employment will decrease because with less consumer spending there is less demand for goods and services, less investment, less production (output) so less demand for labour, less employment. If the increase in interest rates causes the exchange rate to appreciate, and fewer New Zealand goods are sold overseas, there will be less production in New Zealand, so less employment.

One benefit of low inflation is if New Zealand's inflation rate is below that of our trading partners, then New Zealand exports will be relatively more price competitive, so exports will increase (imports to New Zealand will be relatively more expensive), so more export-led growth/demand for New Zealand goods. Therefore, the long-term gains of low inflation will outweigh the short-term costs due to high interest/exchange rates. The main benefit of lower inflation is a stable economy, which allows firms/households to plan with greater certainty/firms more likely to expand/invest/better price signals, which will lead to long-term growth. Therefore the (long-term) gains will outweigh the (short-term) costs due to high interest/exchange rates (such as less demand for goods and services/less growth, etc).

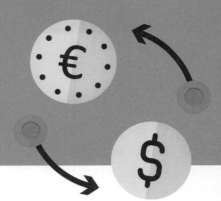

Fiscal policy

The government announces the changes to its income and expenditure in the Budget. Government income comes from various sources including taxation (direct tax and indirect tax), fees, fines and investment income. Taxation policies (along with government spending) form **fiscal policy** that a government uses in order to influence the level of economic activity (aggregate demand). The **operating balance** is calculated by working out the difference between government revenue (income) and government spending or expenses.

Operating balances can often be greater or smaller than forecast because government tax revenues or government expenses (or spending) are liable to change due to economic conditions or events. A major disaster like an earthquake or prolonged drought will increase expenses and reduce revenue, this will make the operating surplus smaller or operating deficit larger. An unexpected boom in tourism will increase revenue as the tax take increases because direct tax receipts increase as employment increases and company profits increase, expenses will fall because fewer benefits are paid to the unemployed. Overall the operating surplus will be greater or an operating deficit smaller.

A tax is a compulsory payment to the government and can be placed on incomes (direct taxes) or expenditure (indirect taxes). Tax is the main means by which the government raises revenue to finance its spending (or expenditure). Tax revenue collected can be used to pay for government debt or be used to redistribute income to reduce the gap between the rich and poor within a country. By changing rates of direct or indirect tax a government can influence the consumption of certain goods and services and either stimulate or dampen economic activity.

During a recession the government will collect less in direct tax because fewer workers are hired (employed) and firms lay off staff or pay less overtime to workers because of reduced output. Business profits decline with fewer sales and revenue. Firms will pay less company tax to the government because profits made are likely to be lower. Government spending on transfer payments will increase because newly unemployed workers now receive a benefit. The government will collect less in indirect tax, such as GST because household consumption spending falls. Government spending in education is likely to increase because more students stay longer at school or go on to university. Overall these effects of a recession will increase an operating deficit or reduce an operating surplus.

       ISBN: 9780170438131

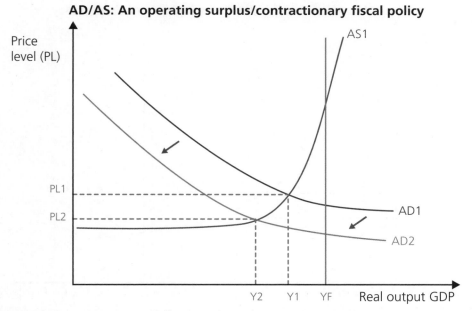

AD/AS: An operating surplus/contractionary fiscal policy

Price level (PL)

AS1

PL1

PL2

AD1

AD2

Y2   Y1   YF   Real output GDP

If the level of economic activity is near capacity, there is likely to be inflationary pressure in the economy, and the government will dampen the level of economic activity by running a budget surplus **(contractionary fiscal policy)**. A budget surplus occurs when the government's income is greater than its expenditure. It could involve a decrease in government spending, decreasing transfer payments and increasing both direct and indirect taxes. Households' disposable incomes will decrease and consumption spending will fall, this will dampen economic activity. As households spend less, firms' inventories (stock levels) are likely to increase, therefore business confidence may fall and firms invest less because they view the risks of new ventures as higher. A fall in investment spending will further dampen economic activity. An **operating surplus** will decrease aggregate demand because government withdrawals (taxes/ income) is greater than government injections (government spending/subsidies) so AD shifts inward/ left (from AD1 to AD2). Overall, an operating surplus will dampen economic activity resulting in a decrease in inflationary pressures (shown as the decrease in the price level from PL1 to PL2) and decrease employment and real output GDP (as shown as the decrease from Y1 to Y2).

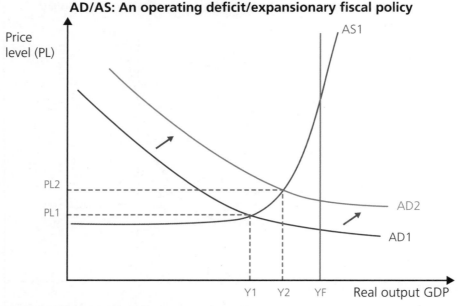

AD/AS: An operating deficit/expansionary fiscal policy

A government **operating (budget) deficit** is where government spending exceeds income. This is **expansionary fiscal policy** that is used during a recession, depression or period of stagnant economic activity where an economy is operating below its full potential. It involves either increasing government spending, increasing transfers or decreasing direct or indirect taxes. An increase in government spending will inject more money into the economy by the funding of new projects such as schools, roads, bridges, hospitals, etc. Firms will hire additional workers or pay existing workers overtime to carry out these projects and are likely to increase investment spending on capital items because they are more confident about the future. Household incomes will increase as more workers are employed, so consumption spending will increase. Overall, as government, consumption and investment spending increase, aggregate demand will increase. An operating deficit will increase aggregate demand because government injections (government spending/subsidies) is greater than government withdrawals (taxes/income) so AD shifts outward/right (from AD1 to AD2). Overall, an operating budget deficit will stimulate economic activity resulting in an increase in inflationary pressures (shown as the increase in the price level from PL1 to PL2) and increase employment and real output GDP (as shown as the increase from Y1 to Y2). The Reserve Bank will hold the OCR at its current level if there is unlikely to be a breach of the Policy Target Agreement. However, if there is going to be a breach in the PTA they are likely to raise the OCR to control inflationary pressures in the economy.

As income (direct) tax rates are reduced then household disposable incomes would increase. Households may decide to spend this or save, therefore the impact on consumption spending (C) is uncertain. Households consumption spending (C) could increase therefore causing aggregate demand (AD) to increase (shift outward). As AD shifts outward the general price level (inflation) will increase, employment will increase (unemployment decrease) and real GDP will also increase. If however households save the increase in disposable incomes that result from the direct tax cuts this may mean no or little change to aggregate demand (AD). Overall the effects on the general price level (inflation), employment and real GDP could be indeterminate.

A budget deficit will require that a government borrows funds to cover the excess of expenses over revenue. Borrowing will add to government debt. The borrowing requires that interest is paid and this will add to expenses in future years, also, at some stage, the borrowed funds must be repaid. Persistent deficits will result in increasing debt and increasing interest payments. Finance costs are the debt servicing costs of the government, they may fall because interest rates fall, or debt is repaid through asset sales, or an exchange rate rise leads to lower interest repayments to foreigners.

The government operating balance deficit that is financed by overseas borrowing in the short term will increase the Balance on Financial Account because government borrowing is an inflow (and outflow when repayments are made). Finance costs on the borrowing will also increase the Current Account deficit, because it is an outflow in the Balance of Income. In the long term this deficit will mean that future financial account inflows will be needed to fund the deficit.

1 **a** What is the name given to the announcement of the government's statement of its intended expenditure and revenues?

The Budget

b List several sources of government revenue. Taxation, fees, fines and profits.

c Tick (✓) the three main areas of government expenditure.

Core government services		Health	✓
Defence		Social Welfare	✓
Education	✓	Transport and communication	
Finance costs		Law and order	

d What is the difference between a 'budget deficit' and debt?

A budget deficit is when government spending is greater than its income (revenue). This requires the government to borrow funds to cover the excess of expenses over revenue. Borrowing will add to government debt. The borrowing requires that interest is paid and this will add to expenses in future years, also, at some stage, the borrowed funds must be repaid. Persistent deficits will result in increasing debt and increasing interest payments.

e Explain why government tax revenues increase in a period of expanding economic activity.

Idea that firms employ more workers or pay existing workers overtime so direct tax receipts rise. Household disposable incomes are likely to rise resulting in increased consumer spending on goods and services, therefore increased tax receipts.

f **(i)** Describe what a budget surplus is.

When government income/revenue/taxation is greater than government spending.

(ii) Is a budget surplus an example of expansionary or contractionary fiscal policy?

Contractionary

g Explain the impact of a budget surplus on inflation.

Impact on inflation: Inflation reduced (note not positive or negative)

Explanation: Budget surplus means less government spending relative to taxation, so aggregate demand decreases and (the rate of) inflation/price level falls.

| Direct tax cuts … | GST to increase |

2 **a** Compare and contrast the effects of tax changes on economic activity.
In your answer you should:

- Describe what is meant by a direct tax and explain the effects of direct tax cuts on the economy.
- Describe what is meant by an indirect tax and explain the effect of an increase in GST.

Direct taxes are taxes levied on income or wealth and are paid directly by the taxpayer (individual or company) to the government, for example, income tax and company tax. Direct tax cuts will increase households' disposable income and consumption spending will increase. Firms will increase output to satisfy the increased demand for goods and services. As aggregate demand increases there will be an increase in the general price level (demand-pull inflation) and increase in Real GDP (growth).

Indirect taxes are collected by a third party and passed on to the government, for example, GST. An increase in GST will cause an increase in the cost of production. As costs increase, profit will decrease and the aggregate supply curve will shift inward (to the left). This will cause the general price level to increase (cost-push inflation), a decrease in Real GDP and, therefore, decreased growth.

b Explain the impact on government tax revenue during a boom.

During a boom the government will collect more in direct tax because more workers are hired (employed) and firms pay overtime to workers because of increased output. Business profits increase with more sales and revenue. Firms will pay more company tax to the government. Government spending on transfer payments will decrease because previously unemployed workers now have a job. The government will collect more in indirect tax, such as GST because household consumption spending increases.

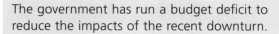

The government has run a budget deficit to reduce the impacts of the recent downturn.

3 a Explain the effects of a budget deficit.

In your answer you should:

- Describe what is meant by a budget deficit and name the type of policy being used by government.
- Explain the likely effect of a budget deficit.
- Explain the likely response of the Reserve Bank to a budget deficit.

A budget deficit is part of government expansionary fiscal policy and occurs when the amount that the government spends is greater than the amount of revenue they collect.

An increase in government spending will inject more money into the economy by the funding of new projects such as schools, roads, bridges, hospitals, etc. Firms will hire additional workers or pay existing workers overtime to carry out these projects and are likely to increase investment spending on capital items as they are more confident about the future. Household incomes will increase as more workers are employed, so consumption spending will increase. Overall, as government, consumption and investment spending increase, aggregate demand will increase. This will cause an increase in the general price level (inflation) and an increase in real output GDP, which is growth. The Reserve Bank will hold the OCR at its current level if there is unlikely to be a breach of the Policy Target Agreement. However, if there is going to be a breach in the PTA they are likely to raise the OCR to control inflationary pressures in the economy.

b (i) What is the name given to a government payment with nothing received in return?

Transfer payment

(ii) Explain how lower Real GDP would impact on revenue and expenditure for the government budget.

Idea: lower Real GDP means lower incomes and lower tax take. Unemployment is likely to increase and result in higher spending on welfare benefits.

> Growth is an objective of government.

4 a (i) Explain the impact of increased government spending on growth.

An increase in government spending will inject more money into the economy because money is spent on new projects. Employment will increase and household income will increase. Consumption spending will increase. Firms are likely to invest more since business confidence is likely to rise. AD will increase causing the PL to go up and so demand-pull inflation will increase, real output GDP will also increase therefore causing economic growth.

(ii) Explain why economic growth is an objective of government.

Growth is an objective of government economic policy because it is one of the keys to higher standards of living. Growth has made it possible for people to achieve better living and working conditions, greater life expectancy and a better way of life. For the government it is desirable because it brings in increasing revenues from a given structure of tax rates. It means that more and better roads, schools, hospitals and other social services can be provided without resorting to raising the rates of taxation. Growth can create greater employment opportunities for individuals and unemployment can fall. Economic growth makes it easier for the government to carry out policies of income redistribution and achieve greater equity of income distribution.

b A boom in economic activity has a positive effect on the revenue collected by the government. State an area of government revenue that will be affected and describe why the revenue collected will increase.

Area of revenue affected: direct tax e.g., P.A.Y.E. or corporate tax. Indirect tax e.g., GST.

Revenue collected will fall because: P.A.Y.E. – more people working or will be working longer hours. Corporate tax – an upturn means greater profit for business. OR – Indirect tax e.g., GST increases because more economic activity means greater spending so more GST is collected.

c Government revenue comes from various sources:

(i) Give an example of a non-tax revenue.

e.g., Fines, fees, interest, SOE profits

(ii) Four areas of expenditure take over 58% of government expenditure. List three of these areas of spending.

Health, education, Social security and welfare, finance costs

d What is meant by expansionary fiscal policy?

An increase in government spending or a decrease in taxes (or both) designed to stimulate economic activity (i.e., increase real GDP).

e Explain the statement 'high rates of economic growth do not promise work for all'.

Idea that not everyone can do every job, so unemployed people and vacancies may not match up. There can be a shortage of labour in some industries and unemployment in others. Growth may be caused by the greater use of capital or existing workers working overtime or being more productive, therefore employment may not change at all.

> Government spending on infrastructure is set to increase. This includes the holiday highway up north and completing the national cycleway.

5 a Compare and contrast the effects of government spending on the economy. Explain the initial impact of government spending on the level of unemployment. Explain the flow-on effects on consumption spending, investment spending and net exports.

The initial impact of government spending would see unemployment decrease because more workers are required to build the cycleway, work on the roads and bridges that flow on from the spending on infrastructure.

Firms associated with the projects undertaken by government will hire additional workers or pay existing workers overtime. Households' disposable income will increase and consumption spending will increase. Aggregate demand will increase, causing an increase in demand-pull inflation and an increase in real output GDP, which is growth.

Investment spending by firms will increase because firms involved in building the infrastructure will be more confident about the future and are likely to need new equipment to assist with work on these projects. Aggregate demand will increase, causing an increase in demand-pull inflation and an increase in real output GDP, which is growth.

As overseas visitor numbers increase during events or because tourists are attracted by the new cycleway, they will spend on goods and services in New Zealand, so export receipts will increase. Aggregate demand will increase, causing an increase in demand-pull inflation and an increase in real output GDP, which is growth.

b Complete the table with a tick (✓) to indicate if the situation outlined is likely to occur when the economy is expanding or contracting.

	Situation	Expanding economy	Contracting economy
(i)	A rise in the number of business closures.		✓
(ii)	A decrease in the number of building consents.		✓
(iii)	An increase in the level of business confidence.	✓	
(iv)	Workers are being made redundant and levels of unemployment are rising.		✓
(v)	Firms are paying workers overtime and there is a scarcity of resources available.	✓	
(vi)	Increased investment by firms and Real GDP is rising.	✓	
(vii)	Firms are recording record sales and company profits rise.	✓	
(viii)	The government operating surplus swells to $2.5b.	✓	
(ix)	The government operating deficit increases from $500m to $3b.		✓

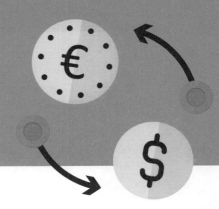

14 MACROECONOMICS
Supply-side policy

Economic growth can be increased by either increasing output from existing resources and/or increasing the quantity of resources available to a country. The discovery of new resources (minerals, fish species) will increase economic growth in the short run. This growth may slow later as these new resources or existing resources are used up or are over exploited.

Productive capacity is a measure of an economy's economic potential (the maximum attainable an economy can produce), rather than looking at the actual output of an economy. The OECD (Organisation for Economic Co-operation and Development) measures 'economic potential' and compares it to the actual performance of an economy in its 'output gaps' statistic. An increase in productive capacity can be illustrated by an outward shift of the production possibility frontier. The use of supply side policies by a government will improve the productive capacity of an economy.

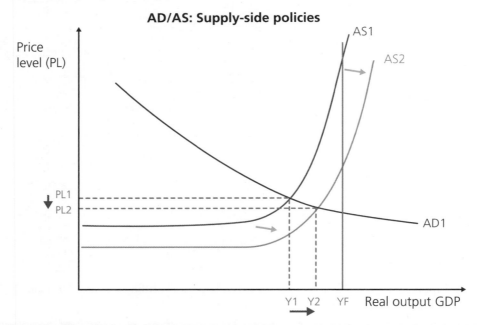

AD/AS: Supply-side policies

The full employment (YF) or long-run aggregate supply curve shows that all resources are fully employed and that firms are working to their capacity. The YF curve will shift outwards when new technology is developed or if new resources are discovered. **Supply-side policies** are intended to increase aggregate supply, as aggregate supply increases there will be in an increase in real output GDP (economic growth) and employment, shown as the increase from Y1 to Y2, while reducing inflationary pressures in an economy, shown as the decrease in the price level from PL1 to PL2. The demand for labour is derived from the level of real output, as production increases due to increased demand, so more workers are required by firms, decreasing unemployment or increasing employment as shown by the movement from Y1 to Y2 on the AD/AS model.

Productivity is a factor that will cause the aggregate supply curve to shift. Productivity is a measure of the efficiency of the production process and refers to the rate of output. It is a measure of output per unit of input; i.e., output divided by input. Productivity of labour is output per worker, i.e., output divided by the number of workers. **Human capital** is the skill and ability of the workforce, acquired through education and experience. The quality of the workforce has a direct impact on the output per worker (or productivity). If the same output is produced at a lower cost than before then productivity has improved. Firms that can increase productivity are able to become more competitive because they are producing more with less.

      ISBN: 9780170438131

Productivity of labour (output per worker) can be improved by training workers, greater specialisation by utilising the division of labour or increased use of technology. Investment in human capital in the form of education and workplace training has the potential to increase the skill level of the workforce in the economy, so productivity improves. Investment in human capital will result in more people able to innovate and develop new ideas and technology, so technology will improve. With increases in productivity and technology the productive capacity of the economy and output will increase, resulting in increased growth.

Higher rates of higher education qualifications either directly provided by the government through schools and universities or with the government assisting education providers can result in a better educated workforce that should result in higher levels of output per worker (productivity). It is likely that with improved productivity a firm's costs fall as the production process becomes more efficient, profits will rise and the aggregate supply curve will shift outwards. Labour market reforms that results in creating greater flexibility in labour markets can increase productivity and output in the economy and encourage growth.

Physical capital refers to the manufactured goods used in production. An increase in physical capital will increase the productive capacity of an economy and improvements in technology will increase productivity. Improved productivity will mean the economy can produce more with the same number of workers, production will increase, therefore growth increases. **Technological advancements** as a consequence of research and development can result in newer and faster ways to produce goods and services, the costs of production to firms will decrease for a given quantity of inputs. A government can encourage research and development by providing tax incentives or breaks or funds in the form of grants which may not be needed to be paid back. As productivity levels increase, firms' costs of production fall. Decreased costs increase profits, so firms plan to produce more at each price level thereby shifting the aggregate supply curve to the right (outward).

Aggregate supply (AS) is total production of all firms in the economy. If there is a **reduction in company tax rates** profits earned by a firm would be taxed at a lower rate and returns made higher for the owners. Therefore, it is likely that new businesses will be encouraged to set up and output in an economy increase. New Zealand Trade and Enterprise is the Government trade and economic development agency that provides a range of services to address the capability and market development needs of businesses throughout their life cycle; from start-ups to internationally competitive exporting companies. Politicians will often promote New Zealand trade interests on visits overseas. These measures are government initiated and funded and can result in firms increasing output to make the most of the resources and opportunities available.

A government will look to maintain and update the **capital stock levels** (rail, roads, bridges, tunnels, internet and the power grid) in the economy by spending on transportation, communication and other infrastructure items that a country requires to function efficiently. Improving the movement of people, information, raw materials or goods and services, that is quicker and avoids delays or errors means that the production process will be more efficient, with productivity levels in an economy rising. An increase in productivity levels in an economy will decrease costs of production. Decreased costs increase profit so the aggregate supply curve shifts outward (to the right) as planned output at each price level rises.

Periods of high economic growth can result in the accelerated use of scarce resources and damage to the environment. In New Zealand the purpose of the Resources Management Act (RMA) is to promote sustainable management of natural and physical resources, so they would not be jeopardised or their use would not have adverse effects on the environment. Input is sought from interested parties involved in any development to address the effects of the proposed activity rather than the activity itself. To obtain a consent may mean that firms wanting to expand or start new projects will find that the risks are greater because of greater uncertainty involved. So production falls or time delays or increased compliance costs leads to lower output and growth because some firms may not proceed with their plans or reduce the size of their ventures. The overall effect on growth is difficult to judge. In the short term economic growth may slow, while in the long term, by ensuring adverse effects on the environment are minimised, sustainable economic growth is feasible.

Reforms that are part of supply-side policies are intended to increase the efficiency of factor inputs used in production process. Governments have taken a more "market-like" approach to handling of economic issues by becoming less involved in providing certain goods and services. Based on the idea that the private sector can be more efficient at providing goods and services such as power generation, health and education, there has seen an increase in the deregulation of industry in many countries. By encouraging efficiency, increasing competition and reducing monopoly power, inflationary pressures can be reduced. If there are increases in productivity there is less pressure on prices as more can be produced at the same cost.

Reducing the rate of inflation has benefits for an economy. A lower inflation rate for a country relative to its trading partners can boost exports, improve its balance of payments position and create a climate of business certainty that encourages long term investment that makes growth sustainable and provides employment opportunities.

As with all government policies supply-side policies have a time delay in their implementation and their impact on aggregate supply and the economy. Training and education programmes that make workers more productive do not happen immediately or overnight. By making an economy more efficient and competitive a country is better placed to be able to compete in overseas markets (exports) and domestic firms more able to face competition from imported goods and services as increases in productivity assist local firms produce goods and services at lower prices.

    ISBN: 9780170438131

Productivity improvements in the New Zealand economy have arisen as government have made Research and Development (R & D) attractive to firms.

1 a Explain the effect that changes in productivity have on inflation and economic growth.

In your answer:

- Illustrate the effects that improved productivity have on the macro economy. Label the curves, any shifts and identify the new equilibrium. Explain the changes you have made to Graph One.

Graph One: AD/AS model

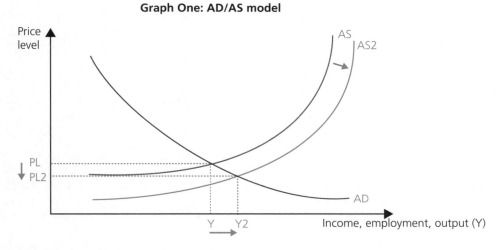

Productivity is output per worker (or machine) and is a determinant of aggregate supply (AS). Increased productivity means that the production process is becoming more efficient. This enables firms to produce more goods and services with the same resources, or decrease the cost of production of producers.

The aggregate supply curve shifts outwards (right) from AS to AS2. This will increase economic growth (shown as the change from Y to Y2) and decrease the price level (shown as the change from PL to PL2).

b Explain the impact of unions seeking a wage increase on inflation and businesses. Explain the impact of wage increases on inflation and how wage increases and inflation will affect employment levels and output of businesses.

In times of inflation, wages may fail to keep pace with the increases in the general price level so real wages fall. Unions will seek wage awards to keep up with inflation which will increase costs to the firm. As costs of production increase, profits decrease and the AS curve shifts inward causing cost-push inflation.

With inflation occurring because of wage increases, firms' costs will increase and the firms will increase prices to retain profit margins. As prices increase the quantity demanded by consumers will fall. Firms may find that stock (inventory) levels build up so they will reduce output and cut back production. As production falls, firms will need fewer resources and they will cut back on workers' hours or even make some workers redundant, therefore employment will fall.

To reduce carbon footprints firms are taking measures to reduce greenhouse gases.

2 a Explain how the increased costs from measures used to reduce greenhouse gases by firms may affect economic growth, inflation and employment. In your answer, on Graph One, show how the increased costs for firms will affect real GDP.

Graph One: AD/AS model of an economy

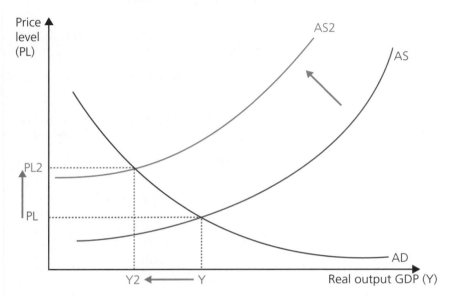

Measures taken by firms to reduce greenhouse gases will increase costs, as costs of production increase then profits will decrease, less will be produced at each price level and the AS curve shifts inward (from AS to AS2). This will decrease real output GDP from Y to Y2 and cause economic growth to decrease.

b Compare and contrast the impact on producers, households and the environment of the change in economic growth resulting from reducing greenhouse gases. In your answer, refer to the changes you made on Graph One and explain the costs and benefits for producers, the costs and benefits for households and the impact on the environment.

The costs to firms of reducing greenhouse gases will be that as costs increase, profits will decrease. Some firms may have to close down. The benefits could be that overseas buyers may increase demand for products that are environmentally friendly, increasing sales, revenue and profits. New markets may open up in these areas.

The costs to households is that prices may rise and there could be job losses as output in the economy falls. The benefits could be more job opportunities in new areas or health aspects that arise from less pollution in the environment or reduced global warming.

The impact on the environment is that carbon emissions, pollution and global warming will decrease as output falls and producers find ways to reduce greenhouse gases.

 ISBN: 9780170438131

3 a Draw a fully labelled AD/AS diagram on the axes below, show a deflationary (recessionary) gap.

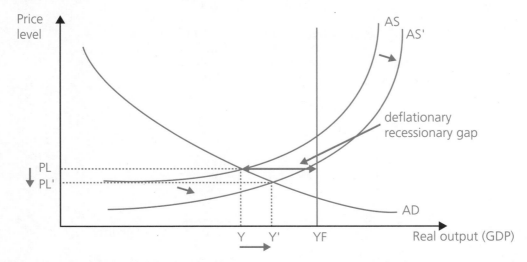

b Labour reforms and deregulation over the last decade are assumed to have made the New Zealand economy more efficient. Show and clearly label the effects of these policies on your diagram.

Employment and output will have increased and prices (price level) decreased.

_____

> The Resource Management Act has an impact on the rate of growth in an economy.

c Explain the effects of the Resource Management Act. In your answer you should:
- Outline the purpose of the Resource Management Act (RMA).
- Explain the possible impact on economic growth of obtaining a resource consent.

The purpose of the Resource Management Act (RMA) is to promote sustainable management of

national and physical resources so they are not jeopardised or their use does not have adverse effects

on the environment.

_____

The Resource Management Act might restrict growth because of increasing costs to firms. To obtain a

consent may mean that firms wanting to expand or start new projects will find that the risks are greater

because of greater uncertainty involved. So production falls/time delays or compliance costs/restricting

resource use which leads to lower production/output and growth. Some firms may not proceed with

their plans or reduce the size of their ventures. While the time delay in obtaining a resource consent

could slow growth in the short term, it may make sustainable economic growth feasible in the long

term.

_____

_____

_____

_____

_____

4 a On Graph One, show the impact of a net migration loss. Explain the effect that a net migration loss has on economic growth. Refer to Graph One in your answer.

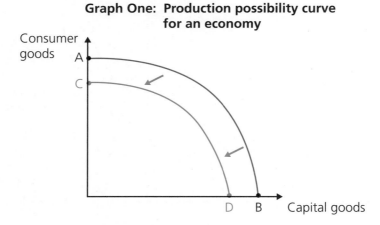

Graph One: Production possibility curve for an economy

A net migration loss will shift the PPC inward (from AB to CD) because it will reduce the productive capacity of an economy because there are fewer labour resources. This will mean that the potential output that the economy is capable of will decrease, economic growth will decline as a result.

b Discuss the impact of the change in economic growth resulting from a net migration loss.
- explain the costs and benefits of the changes in economic growth to households
- explain how the impacts on households would affect businesses and the government
- explain the likely combined impact of the changes you have described above.

Households will benefit because they will face less competition in the labour market when seeking a job and property prices may fall due to a decrease in demand and increase in supply as individuals move overseas. The cost to households could be that as firms reduce output due to decreased demand they need fewer workers, so lay off staff. There could be fewer job opportunities and less choice as the demand for goods and services falls.

Businesses may reduce output because with fewer individuals to buy goods and services demand decreases. Firms' incomes are likely to fall and profitability will fall. Firms are likely to lay off staff and decide to cut back on investment plans. The government will collect less in direct tax because fewer workers are employed and will have to increase transfer payments. As consumption spending falls government will collect less individual tax from firms. Reduced government revenue will possibly result in less spending elsewhere.

The combined effect of reduced consumption spending by households and investment spending by businesses will result in AD shifting inward and decrease real output GDP (economic growth).

Increases in physical capital and human capital
both play a part in determining growth.

5 a Explain how resources affect growth. In your answer you should:
- Define physical capital and human capital.
- Explain how an increase in physical capital affects economic growth.
- Explain how investment in human capital can impact on growth.

Physical capital refers to the manufactured goods used in production. Human capital is the skill and

ability of the workforce, acquired through education and experience.

An increase in physical capital will increase the productive capacity of an economy and improvements in

technology will increase productivity. Improved productivity will mean the economy can produce more

with the same number of workers, production will increase, therefore growth increases.

Investment in human capital in the form of education and workplace training has the potential to

increase the skill level of the workforce in the economy, so productivity improves. Investment in human

capital will result in more people able to innovate and develop new ideas and technology, so technology

will improve. With increases in productivity and technology the productive capacity of the economy and

output will increase, resulting in increased growth.

b (i) Show the effect of a nominal interest rate increase on the New Zealand economy. Label any
curve shifts, and label the new equilibrium price level PL2 and the new equilibrium level of real
output Y2.

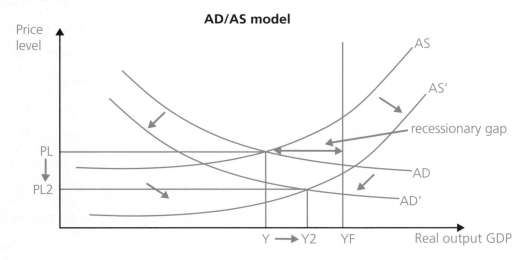

(ii) Based on your graph indicate what will be the effect of an increase in nominal interest rates
on: (Circle your answer).

(1) Inflation	Increase	**Decrease**	No change
(2) Economic growth	**Increase**	Decrease	No change
(3) Unemployment	Increase	**Decrease**	No change

(iii) Explain your answer for unemployment above.

Should discuss the idea that demand for labour is derived from the level of real output. E.g., Real

GDP means more output produced so more labour needed (i.e., (derived) demand for labour rises,

decreasing unemployment or increasing the amount of employment. Answer must relate to the

graph.

Growth has both costs and benefits for society.

6 Compare and contrast the costs and benefits of economic growth.

In your answer you should:

- Explain the positive effects of growth.
- Explain the negative effects of growth.

Positive effects of growth are that as real output GDP increases and firms hire additional workers to satisfy the increase in demand there will be lower levels of unemployment and therefore fewer social problems and less poverty. New technology used to create growth should improve working conditions, reduce the working week and increase leisure time. Government tax revenue should increase and with less welfare spending on unemployment benefits, government can increase its spending in other areas such as health and education. Household incomes should increase and should lead to an increase in the material standard of living. As growth increases, job opportunities may allow workers to seek new job opportunities or challenges where they arise.

The negative effects of growth that come about because of the increase in output could be the accelerated use of scarce resources may mean the growth and standard of living of future generations may be affected as non-renewable (irreplaceable) resources are used up. Certain types of economic activity may have a detrimental effect on the environment. The waste and pollution generated can destroy native habitats for endangered plants and animals, and toxins can threaten health and life. Global warming impacts on sea levels and may result in climate changes. As the size of the ozone hole increases the incidence of skin cancer increases and damage to agricultural crops and plankton in the world's oceans increases.

The new technology used in achieving growth may result in jobs disappearing or with workers being replaced. Workers may have to seek new opportunities in other parts of the country, possibly disrupting family life. Higher incomes that may arise with economic growth may result in greater income inequality. As the rich get richer and the poor, poorer, this may create stress and social tension because individuals attempt to keep up with what society expects. Rates of heart disease and obesity can increase as individuals over-indulge due to higher incomes.

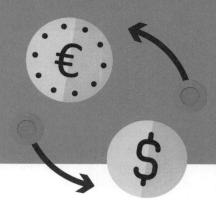

The name given to government measures that impede or inhibit the free flow of goods and services between nations is termed **protectionism**. Impediments to trade between countries may take the form of tariffs, quotas or other restrictions. **Free trade** is where trade between countries occurs without government interference.

The following are a few of the arguments for protectionism. The **infant industry argument** is based on the idea that protection may be necessary while an industry develops until it eventually becomes competitive and able to compete against established foreign competitors. Without protection the infant industry may be unable to withstand the competition and be forced to close down. The **strategic (essential industry) argument** is that certain industries are regarded as vital to a nation at war, e.g., iron and steel, agriculture and chemicals. Given this, it is desirable that such industries be preserved in the interests of national security. The **employment argument** is based along the lines that the entry of cheaper imported products may cause domestic firms to close down, with workers losing their jobs. Trade barriers will protect workers' jobs by reducing consumer spending on imported goods.

A **tariff** is a tax placed (or levied) on imports that raises the price of imported goods thereby making locally-made products relatively more price competitive. This may protect jobs and/or improve the balance of payments but it can cause resentment overseas. High tariffs on imports may cause a country's trading partners to retaliate and follow suit by placing tariffs on exports of foreign made goods. As trading partners import fewer goods and services (meaning that exports fall) then jobs may be lost both in the short run and the long run. This is because a decrease in output means fewer resources are needed, with firms hiring fewer workers or laying off staff. Some firms may close down with subsequent jobs losses. Further unemployment may occur in firms that provide resources or services to the export industries that cease operating due to the fall in sales. High tariffs may protect workers' jobs but it may cause industries to become less efficient because of a lack of competition.

The philosophy that the market provides the best signals for efficient resource use, subsidies and import protection are looked upon as interference with the free working of the market. It follows that any interference with market forces leads to the preservation of relatively inefficient productive units within both export and domestic sectors. The elimination of subsidies and controls will lead to the closure of inefficient units and a shift of resources to areas of more efficient production. While there is an opportunity cost in terms of lost production and short-term unemployment, there is a money cost in subsidies and administering import licensing schemes, though tariffs are revenue-producing. Money costs are a drain on government revenue. Firms must compete in international markets and therefore must be competitive in terms of production and selling costs and therefore of pricing. Shedding inefficient units is a way of making the export sector in a country more competitive. Inefficient domestic producers reliant on import protection for survival can penalise the domestic consumer in terms of price, quality and choice of goods. The high price of imports due to tariff protection also penalises the consumer. Therefore, government **trade reforms** in many countries have involved a shift from protectionist policies to being free trade.

Measures taken result in the removal of subsidies and the phasing out and lowering of tariffs to liberalise trade. Domestic firms have to become more competitive and efficient to survive and able to compete with cheaper imported goods and services. As a result, resources shift from sectors and industries of the economy that are not internationally competitive, and into sectors or industries that are. Industries have to adapt, become more efficient and take advantage of new opportunities either domestically or overseas. While there are job losses in some sectors and industries in the short run there can be job opportunities arising in other sectors in the long run as change takes place. Free trade is likely to see exports increase because greater access to new or existing markets can increase sales for export related industries. Firms that increase sales will require more workers so jobs are created while an increase in export receipts can improve a country's current account position. In many countries the production of goods and services often requires the importing of essential resources or machinery available from an overseas supplier. By removing tariffs the costs of these raw materials or components falls, as costs of production fall profits will increase and the aggregate supply curve shifts outward (to the right) as planned output increases.

QUESTIONS & TASKS

The removal of tariffs is in New Zealand's best interest.

1 Compare and contrast the effects of the removal of tariffs.

In your answer you should:

- Explain the negative effects of the removal of tariffs.
- Explain the positive effects of the removal of tariffs.
- Draw a conclusion if the removal of tariffs is in New Zealand's best interest.

The negative effects of removing tariffs are that some New Zealand firms will be unable to compete with cheaper imports and will close down. Some workers will lose their jobs. Social and economic effects of higher unemployment. Greater income inequality.

The positive effects of removing tariffs include increased economic growth. More trading opportunities overseas if other countries also remove trade barriers. Cheaper imports for consumers. Lower inflation. More imports means a wider range of products for consumers. Resources will be reallocated to industries where we have a comparative advantage. New Zealand producers forced to become more efficient.

In conclusion, the positive effects of New Zealand exporting more will outweigh the negative effect of more imports because the rest of the world is a large market compared with New Zealand. Therefore, the increase in sales of exports to the rest of the world will be considerably more than the increase in imports from the rest of the world, so the overall impact is a good one. The removal of tariffs is a good policy because resources will be reallocated to industries where New Zealand has a comparative advantage, rather than remaining in inefficient industries which rely on government protection to survive. The industries where New Zealand has a comparative advantage will be able to compete in the large world markets, and the potential growth in these industries will outweigh any negative effects that occur from removing the tariffs.

> The signing of a free trade agreement has an impact on both exports and imports.

2 Explain the effects of signing a free trade agreement on the macro-economy goals of full employment and a balanced current account.

In your answer:

* Illustrate the likely effects of signing a free trade agreement. Label the curves and identify equilibrium points.
* Explain how signing a free trade agreement could result in full employment and a balanced current account.

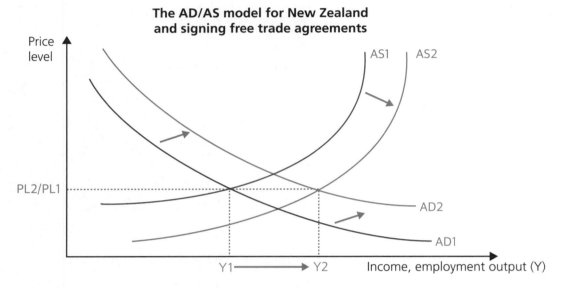

The AD/AS model for New Zealand and signing free trade agreements

Signing a free trade agreement will make it easier for New Zealand firms to export goods and services to overseas markets because trade barriers are relaxed or removed. This will increase export receipts and increase AD (AD1 to AD2). The cost of imports will fall, reducing firms' costs of production. As costs fall, profits increase and increase AS (AS1 to AS2). It is likely that the increase in export receipts is greater than the increase in import payments, therefore the current account is likely to be a smaller deficit, moving it closer to zero.

As export firms increase production to satisfy greater demand from overseas, firms hire additional workers. This reduces unemployment. Some workers may lose jobs in industries where cheaper imported products compete with domestically-produced products. However, since New Zealand has had an open economy for a long period of time, the impact of a new free trade agreement may be slight. Overall, it is likely that employment will increase (as shown by the change from Y1 to Y2). However, there is likely to be unemployment in other New Zealand industries that are not related to trade.

3 Rewrite the following statements to identify if they are an argument for free trade or an argument for protectionism in the space provided below.

Prevent dumping	Strategic reason
Lower prices	Protect local employment
Resources will be used more efficiently	Greater range of products for consumers
Allow infant industry to develop	Can increase exports
Tariff revenue for government	

Argument for free trade:

Lower prices, greater range of products for consumers, resources will be used more efficiently, can increase exports.

Argument for protectionism:

Protect local employment, allow infant industry to develop, prevent dumping, strategic reason, tariff revenue for government.

Which would be better for the New Zealand economy in the future, greater free trade or increased protectionism? Justify your answer.

Either answer can be valid. The government should continue to promote free trade because the advantages to New Zealand in terms of increased access to export markets, lower prices and a greater range of goods for consumers, etc, outweigh the costs of job losses and firm closures in industries that are unable to compete with overseas producers. OR, the government should increase protectionism for New Zealand firms in order to keep industries in New Zealand, so more jobs are available, a greater range of goods are produced here, and we do not become dependent on goods manufactured overseas.

> Free trade is where trade between countries occurs without government intervention. The opposite occurs when a government seeks to inhibit or restrict trade with other nations.

4 Explain the policies that involve trade without government intervention.

In your answer you should:

- State the name of the policy that impedes trade and list measures that it may involve.
- Explain reasons for government adopting measures to restrict trade.
- Describe what a Free Trade Agreement is.
- Explain arguments put forward to allow free trade to occur.

The name of the policy that impedes trade between countries is protectionism. Measures that a government could use to impede trade with other nations include tariffs, import licenses or quotas, embargoes, red tape.

Reasons that a government may give for adopting measures that restrict trade include the following.

Infant industry argument: protection may be necessary while an industry develops until it eventually becomes competitive and able to compete against established foreign competitors.

Without protection the infant industry may be unable to withstand the competition and be forced to close down.

Strategic (essential industry) reasons: certain industries are regarded as vital to a nation at war, e.g. iron and steel, agriculture and chemicals. Given this, it is desirable that such industries be preserved in the interests of national security.

Employment: the entry of cheaper imported products may cause firms to close down, with workers losing their jobs. Trade barriers will protect workers' jobs by reducing spending on imported goods.

A Free Trade Agreement is an arrangement between countries to remove trade barriers between them.

Arguments for a government to allow free trade to occur are that free trade allows producers to gain access to a wider range of markets and consumers a wider range of products at lower prices. Free trade has the advantage of allowing countries to make the best use of scarce resources from specialisation. It makes sense for countries to specialise in certain products that they are best suited to producing and to buy products that they could possibly only produce at a higher cost.

    ISBN: 9780170438131

5 Compare and contrast the impact that signing a free trade agreement (FTA) could have on various money flows in the circular flow model and on economic growth.

In your answer:

- explain how the withdrawal flow associated with the government sector would be affected by a growth in exports associated with a free trade agreement
- explain the money flow that would be directly affected in the circular flow model diagram by signing a free trade agreement
- explain how economic growth could result from signing a free trade agreement.

The withdrawal flow associated with the government sector is taxes (direct and indirect). The government would receive more direct tax because export growth would result in jobs and more workers being employed. Some workers would move into higher tax brackets and pay more tax. Businesses that export would earn higher incomes and make greater profits and pay more company/direct tax. There would be increased spending by households as incomes increase and the government would receive more indirect tax (GST) revenue.

Export receipts would increase with signing a FTA because exporters would be selling more goods and services to overseas buyers/consumers. Import payments would increase because New Zealand consumers would be buying more goods and services from producers in overseas countries.

The increased demand for goods and services by overseas buyers would result in New Zealand firms producing more to satisfy demand, employment will increase because firms will need additional workers to produce the new output. The increase in output will mean that economic growth is happening.

With increased exports, firms would become more confident about the future and perceive the risks of investment to be lower. As investment increases, AD would increase and result in an increase in real output GDP (economic growth). The cost of imported raw materials for firms would fall because the tariff on them is removed. Lower costs of production would increase profitability and result in the AS curve shifting outwards. This would result in an increase in real output GDP (economic growth).

ISBN: 9780170438131